WRITE YOUR OWN

HISTORICAL FICTION

STORY

by Tish Farrell

First published in the United States in 2006 by
Compass Point Books
151 Good Counsel Drive
P.O. Box 669
Mankato, MN 56002-0669
www.capstonepub.com

Copyright © ticktock Entertainment Ltd 2006
First published in Great Britain in 2006 by ticktock Media Ltd.,
ISBN 1 86007 532 0 PB

 This book was manufactured with paper containing
at least 10 percent post-consumer waste.

For Compass Point Books
Sue Vander Hook, Nick Healy, Anthony Wacholtz, Nathan Gassman, James Mackey,
Abbey Fitzgerald, Catherine Neitge, Keith Griffin, and Carol Jones

For ticktock Entertainment Ltd
Graham Rich, Elaine Wilkinson, John Lingham,
Suzy Kelly, Heather Scott, Jeremy Smith

Library of Congress Cataloging-in-Publication Data
Farrell, Tish.
  Write your own historical fiction story / by Tish Farrell.
     p. cm.—(Write your own)
  Includes bibliographical references and index.
  Audience: Grade 4-6.
  ISBN-13: 978-0-7565-1640-6 (hardcover)
  ISBN-13: 978-0-7565-1815-8 (paperback)
  1. Historical fiction—Authorship—Juvenile literature. I. Title. II. Series.
  PN3377.5.H57F37 2006
  808.3'81—dc22   2005030729

Printed in the United States of America in Stevens Point, Wisconsin.
082010
005926R

Your writing journey

Do you have a passion for the past? If you long to bring historical events to life in your own stories, this book will show you how. You will learn to write your own historical fiction, which lets characters from your imagination encounter real people and events from the past. Your stories can have a sort of energy not found in history books. Now get ready to fire up your time machine and journey back in time.

CONTENTS

WANT TO BE A WRITER?

This book is the perfect place to start. It aims to give you the tools to write your own historical fiction. Learn how to craft believable characters and perfect plots with satisfying beginnings, middles, and endings. Examples from famous books appear throughout, with tips and techniques from published authors to help you on your way.

Get the writing habit

Do timed and regular practice. Real writers learn to write even when they don't particularly feel like it.

Create a story-writing zone.

Keep a journal.

Keep a notebook—record interesting events and note how people behave and speak.

Generate ideas

Find a character whose story you want to tell. What is his or her problem?

Brainstorm to find out everything about your character.

Research settings, events, and other characters.

Get a mix of good and evil characters.

GETTING STARTED · SETTING THE SCENE | CHARACTERS · VIEWPOINT

You can follow your progress by using the bar located on the bottom of each page. The orange color tells you how far along the story-writing process you have gotten. As the blocks are filled out, your story will be growing.

Plan

What is your story about?

What happens?

Plan beginning, middle, and end.

Write a synopsis or create story-boards.

Write

Write the first draft, then put it aside for a while.

Check spelling and dialogue—does it flow?

Remove unnecessary words.

Does the story have a good title and satisfying ending?

Avoid clichés.

Publish

Write or print the final draft.

Always keep a copy for yourself.

Send your story to children's magazines, Internet writing sites, competitions, or school magazines.

SYNOPSES AND PLOTS   WINNING WORDS   SCINTILLATING SPEECH   HINTS AND TIPS   THE NEXT STEP

When you get to the end of the bar, your book is ready to go! You are an author!
You now need to decide what to do with your book and what your next project should be.
Perhaps it will be a sequel to your story, or maybe something completely different.

BEGIN YOUR BLAST TO THE PAST

Historical-story writers transport their readers back in time by the power of their words. The first thing you need to do to succeed is gather your writing materials and find a good place to work. All you need is a pen and paper. A computer can make writing quicker, but it is not essential.

What you need

As a historical-fiction writer you'll need to delve into the past—at your local museum, library, or on the Internet. To help organize your findings, you may find the following useful:

- a small notebook that you carry everywhere
- plenty of scrap paper for writing practice
- pencils and pens for drawing ancient maps and timelines
- Post-it notes to mark reference book pages
- stick-on stars for highlighting key information in your research notes
- files to keep your fact-finding organized and story ideas safe

- index cards for recording key facts
- dictionary, thesaurus, and encyclopedia
- a good general history book to check basic facts
- a camera to record any historic sites you visit

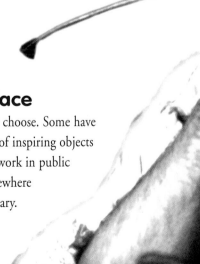

Your writing place

Writers can work where they choose. Some have writing cottages or home offices with lots of inspiring objects around them. Some work in basements; others work in public places, like coffee shops. Experiment. Find somewhere comfortable—perhaps your bedroom or the library. Perhaps your local museum has just the right creative feeling.

Create a story-writing zone

- Play music from your favorite historical period.
- Have some historical images laid out around you.

- Put on a hat that you only wear when you're writing (make one or adapt one you already have).
- Choose intriguing objects for your desk—an old family photograph, a war medal, a shard of ancient pottery, an arrowhead— anything that has a story to tell.

Writer's golden rule

Once you have chosen your writing space, the first step in becoming a writer is: Go there as often as possible and write. You must write and write regularly. This is the writer's golden rule.

Until you are sitting at your desk with pen in hand, no writing can happen. It doesn't matter what you write—an e-mail or a diary entry will do— as long as you write something.

Before you can bring the past to life in historical fiction, you must get into training. The best writers practice writing every day, even when they don't feel inspired. So train as you would to be an athlete!

Now it's your turn

Great events

Sit at your desk, close your eyes, and take four deep breaths. Now open your eyes and write "The Boston Tea Party" at the top of the page. Then brainstorm. See how many other historical events, phrases, and names you can scribble down in two minutes. Write every thought that comes to mind.

TIPS AND TECHNIQUES

Despite a peasants' revolt or the fall of Rome, keep your date with your desk. Even two minutes' practice a day is better than none.

Now it's your turn

A slice of time

Think about your favorite historical event (you probably mentioned it in the brainstorming exercise on page 8). Imagine a time machine has taken you back there. Close your eyes and try to visualize it. What can you feel, hear, smell, touch, and see? Take 10 minutes to write down all your first thoughts. Don't worry about writing complete sentences. Scribble down every impression, even if it seems silly. This is about becoming a writer, not about being the best writer.

When you've finished, give yourself a gold star. You have unlocked your long-lost story archive. The more you do this, the easier it will be to overcome the Story Executioner— your internal critic that always finds fault with your writing.

Case study

In 1930, Laura Ingalls Wilder couldn't find a publisher for her autobiography Pioneer Girl, so she used parts of it to create the first of the much-loved Little House books—Little House in the Big Woods. This story is based on Laura's pioneering life in the big woods of Wisconsin during the late 19th century. Because the writer changed some of the facts, it is called historical fiction rather than autobiography.

Mark Twain and Charles Dickens (left) were not historical-fiction writers. They wrote about their own times. But their books may help you "tune in" to the ways people thought, talked, and lived in the past.

Your own historical fiction

You can bring the past to life through characters created in your own imagination. Historical fiction usually blends facts about the past with imagined stories and characters. Your characters—whether they are gladiators engaged in brutal battles, pioneer children facing the struggles of the frontier, or innocent people forced into prison camps during World War II—can encounter real people and events from the past. But in historical fiction the outcome is uncertain until the story's ending, creating a sort of drama and energy not found in history books.

Read, read, read!

Reading will help you decide which period you most want to write about and should spark ideas. Jot them down in a notebook.

Now it's your turn

Gaining inspiration

Reread your favorite historical-fiction novel. Imagine you are writing it. Look at how the writer uses specific historical details to bring the past to life. Make notes on your thoughts. Copy down one or two of your favorite passages. Underline the details that make a scene work. Try to sketch out what you are reading. Ask yourself if you understand the scene better by drawing it. Did it give you any new ideas about what was happening?

GETTING STARTED   SETTING THE SCENE   CHARACTERS   VIEWPOINT

Case study

Joseph Bruchac writes historical novels that show the important place of Native Americans in American history. Much of his writing draws on his Abenaki ancestry. His American Indian heritage is just one part of an ethnic background that includes Slovak and English blood, but it is the element that has shaped his life the most.

Make notes

Grow your imagination. But if you are not enjoying a book, leave it and start another. Make a note of why you didn't like it. You might find this information useful later. Read some nonfiction history books, too.

TIPS AND TECHNIQUES

As you read, think about whose story you want to tell. In which time and place do the characters live? Record all ideas in your notebook so you will have plenty to draw from for your own story.

Reading lots of good books will help you discover your own writer's voice, which is your own style of writing. It takes most writers a long time to develop their own unique voice.

A writer's voice

Once you start reading as a would-be writer, you'll see that writers have their own rhythm and range of language that stays the same throughout the book. Karen Cushman (*Catherine, Called Birdy*) writes quite differently from Harry Mazer (*A Boy at War*), and Kevin Crossley-Holland (*The Seeing Stone*) writes nothing like Michael Cadnum (*The Leopard Sword*), even though they both write about people going to war in the Middle Ages.

Historic voices

As a writer of historical stories, don't be tempted to use old-fashioned language. Readers quickly tire of too many unfamiliar words. Instead, occasionally use terms from the period, such as personal greetings, to suggest a particular time.

Experiment

For storytelling ideas, try reading other genres. Caroline Lawrence (The Roman Mysteries series) sets her detective stories in ancient Rome. Legends might inspire you, too, as they did Kevin Crossley-Holland in the Arthur series.

WRITERS' VOICES

Look at the following extracts. Not all of them use old-fashioned phrasing, but can you spot the verbal clues the others use to suggest a past time?

1665, Derbyshire, England

A parcel of patterns brought the Plague to Eyam. A parcel sent up from London to George Vicars, a journeyman tailor. ... This was the common report and credence amongst us, though I heard later that the Plague was at Derby at the time when it reached us.

Jill Paton Walsh, *A Parcel of Patterns*

1850s, Mississippi

Julilly ached with tiredness and hunger gnawed wildly at her stomach. ... The other slave girls along the floor slept heavily, but Liza was restless.

"You is a friend," the crippled girl whispered. "No one else ever picked the high cotton that my poor ol' back won't stretch to."

Barbara Smucker, *Runaway to Freedom*

World War II, England

When Chas awakened, the air-raid shelter was silent. Grey winter light was creeping round the door-curtain. It could have been any time. His mother was gone, and the little brown attaché case with the insurance policies and bottle of brandy for emergencies. The all-clear must have gone.

Robert Westall, *The Machine Gunners*

1870s, Missouri

Well, I catched my breath and most fainted. Shut up on a wreck with such a gang as that! But it warn't no time to be sentimentering. We'd got to find that boat now-had to have it for ourselves.

Mark Twain, *Huckleberry Finn*

To write historical fiction, you must be a good storyteller and a determined history detective. It may help to start by writing a story set during a time period you have studied at school.

Start from what you know

Look through your past school assignments—maybe having to do with the ancient Egyptians or the Middle Ages. Start looking for your hero. Search for a dilemma. What is happening in your character's world that is causing big problems?

How one writer found her story

Patricia Curtis Pfitsch says the idea for *Riding the Flume* came from reading a nonfiction book about sequoia trees. The controversial cutting of the trees was just the sort of conflict a storyteller needs. Out of her research into the issue grew the character Francie. This is part of the plot summary from the book's back cover:

> *During the summer of 1894, the giant sequoia trees—the oldest living things on earth—are being felled for lumber in northern California. Francie finds a note in a hole of an old sequoia stump and recognizes her sister's handwriting. But Carrie died in an accident six years earlier. Could the secret still be important? Francie is determined to find out.*
> from *Riding the Flume* by Patricia Curtis Pfitsch

Now it's your turn

Turn fact to fiction

You are in a plague-ridden city of the mid-1600s. The sick are locked in their houses. Men with carts collect the dead. Dogcatchers round up stray animals. Pretend you are a lost spaniel. How do you survive on the streets? How do you escape the dogcatcher? For historical details, read Kathryn Hinds' *Life in the Middle Ages: The City.*

Research is not the full story

Historical research gives you details of places, events, and human conflicts. The historical-fiction writer's art is to shape them into a gripping personal story. For example, in *Riding the Flume,* the main story isn't about cutting sequoias. It is about Francie and her reaction to the tree cutting.

Readers are involved with her dilemmas. They want to know how she will save some of the sequoias, how she will solve the mystery of her dead sister, and if she will have the courage to ride the flume. The research helps writers to create a believable and exciting tale.

The home front

Many historical-story writers start out by basing their stories on their own family's history. Quiz older family members for their memories. There may be old photo albums, wills, family recipes, or letters. This evidence from your own family's past may "speak" to you in surprising ways.

Case study

Mildred D. Taylor (Roll of Thunder, Hear My Cry) was born in Mississippi, the great-granddaughter of a white plantation owner and a slave. She grew up listening to her father's stories about slavery. Years later, when she was trying to tell her grandmother's story about the felling of trees on their family land, the strong-willed character of Cassie Logan emerged, leading to Mildred's books about the Logan family in 1930s America.

Back to basics

Go back to the exercise you did on page 9, writing down your thoughts about a historical event. Did you have any problems—details you didn't know about dress, transport, or the way of life? Perhaps you put in things that hadn't been invented yet—a wristwatch, a skateboard, or a computer? This is easily done, so don't worry.

Now it's your turn

Every picture tells a story

Take a break from writing. Capture the past in drawings. Make a scrapbook or collage of everyday life in your chosen historical time. Download images from the Internet or ask the librarian if you can photocopy some pictures from books. Pictures give you something concrete to describe in stories. Visit your museum and draw interesting objects. If you are allowed to touch them, go for it! Find out what it's like to hold an old pistol or turn a butter churn.

Check out facts in your library and museum

Family history is often patchy—people forget things or remember them incorrectly.

So head for the library and ask the librarian what kinds of historical documents you can consult.

- Old newspapers on microfilm can tell you a lot about the way of life.

- Maps and directories show how your town grew.

- Census records note who lived where and how they made a living.

- Church and government records note births, marriages, and deaths.

Organize the facts

Use index cards to record facts and where you found them. Three-ring binders with plastic sleeves are good for storing pictures and newspaper clippings.

LIVE IN THE PAST

In historical stories the setting must be accurate, and it must include the time and the place. Don't overload your story with details, however. It's like preparing a stage for a play—just the right props must be there for the actors to perform their parts, but there shouldn't be a lot of extras.

Common experiences

Think about how it feels to visit another country or an unfamiliar part of your own city or state. What do you notice most? Is it the shops and the streets, or the way people talk, dress, and look? Do you notice different food, vehicles, or houses? Readers will be interested in those sorts of details from a past time. Those simple details can make your story seem real.

Now it's your turn

Hysterical history

Take a break from research. Throw facts to the wind. For 10 minutes, brainstorm your ideal past. Choose all your favorite bits of history and mix their clothes, buildings, places, times, transportation, people, and events. Samurai girl meets King Tut? Cool!

Now it's your turn

Start up your time machine!

Imagine you are a tour operator who does guided time-machine trips to your chosen past. Plan your route around your setting. Write a few paragraphs about it. Sketch the tour highlights of your created historical world—maybe it's a trip up the Nile in a papyrus reed boat, a look inside a medicine man's home, a nighttime walk along the Great Wall of China, or a glimpse of the frontier hangman's noose. Doing this exercise will help you spot gaps in what you know about your own setting.

Create the setting

Once you have researched enough facts, creating the setting is somewhat like doing a jigsaw puzzle. If you choose only the most vivid, interesting details that affect your characters and plot, your readers should be able to fill in the rest of the picture.

TIPS AND TECHNIQUES

Step into your characters' shoes. As you go back in time, differences between rich and poor peoples' lives may be striking. There was far less freedom in every area of life. Values have changed, too. Behavior that we find shocking now might have been acceptable then, and certainly actions we accept today would have been outrageous in many eras of the past.

How will you transport your readers back in time? Consider how to bring the past to life in ways that readers can easily relate to. Show what your characters feel.

Choose an authentic setting

In Jill Paton Walsh's *A Parcel of Patterns*, the simple need to eat shows the historical setting. Eyam villagers are confined to their settlement so they won't spread the plague. Food deliveries to the village boundary chart the plague's course:

> The Duke sent still the bread and bacon ... to us in ample quantity, soon more by far than the living could eat up. So we took less, and left some lying at the boundary-stones. ... And the sight of the spare loaves lying struck chill into the hearts of the Duke's servants.
>
> Jill Paton Walsh, *A Parcel of Patterns*

TIPS AND TECHNIQUES

Show historical situations from the main character's viewpoints. Make them personal. Be specific—the dead rat stink in the dungeon or the roast hog juices dribbling down a hero's chin.

GETTING STARTED   SETTING THE SCENE   CHARACTERS   VIEWPOINT

Now it's your turn

Ace adjectives

Read the quote on page 20 aloud. Notice how the verbs and adjectives bring the place to life. Now write a scene from your story. Show your hero scaling a wall, pushing through a market, or running away. Use his or her movement through a specific place to create the setting.

Add some action

Mesh the setting with some quick action. In V.A. Richardson's *The House of Windjammer*, it is 1636. The hero, Adam, is dashing through Amsterdam's streets, late for his meeting with his tutor.

> *He cut up between the warehouses and into the squeeze of the alleys and streets. Here the streets burrowed between top-heavy houses that sagged under the weight of their upper floors and roofs. At every turn more streets and alleys opened to the left and right, filled with smoke of fires and the belch of pewter factories. Through the maze of sounds and smells ... he picked his way until he ran straight into trouble.*
>
> V.A. Richardson, *The House of Windjammer*

DISCOVER YOUR HERO

When creating your characters, you must start with the historical facts. Your protagonist, or hero, will be shaped by the times he or she lives in, just as you are. But to make a good story, the character must challenge the system in some way.

Build character

Once you know your hero's problems, you can start shaping him or her into a real person. Regard your hero as a new friend. Ask what he or she wants for a better life. How will he or she get it? What if he or she fails? Find out your hero's likes and dislikes. What are his or her strengths and weaknesses? Can they add drama to the story?

Find a good name

Names come in and out of fashion, so take care. Your Victorian maid won't be called Kylie. Biblical names like Jacob or Job were common in the past. Graveyards and old newspapers are good places to look. Once you have a name, find ways to make your hero sympathetic. If you don't really like him or her, your readers won't either. This is another reason for giving your hero some flaws. No one likes a perfect person.

Now it's your turn

Rough justice?

Brainstorm about your feelings. For seven minutes, write about how it felt when you were betrayed, bullied, or unfairly accused. Then write for seven minutes from the point of view of the person who hurt you. You now have some raw materials to help you create your characters' feelings.

Give them a past

Even historical heroes need some history, just enough to explain their current situation. In *Stop the Train*, Geraldine McCaughrean briefly describes pioneer Cissie's old life as she thinks of the new life she has ahead. If your hero has a complicated past, it could be told in a flashback scene, in conversation with a friend, or perhaps as a short prologue, which introduces your story.

> *It had to be better than the filthy rooming-house they had left behind in Arkansas, with its rats in the basement and flies in the milk.*
>
> Geraldine McCaughrean, *Stop the Train*

Decide what they look like

In real life, people don't often describe themselves directly, so if your hero is your narrator, you may have to be sly in delivering this information. You could get your hero to describe himself or herself as he or she looks into a mirror or as he or she puts on clothes for a special occasion. Or another character could comment on the hero's appearance in dialogue.

TIPS AND TECHNIQUES

If you can't imagine what your hero looks like, search old pictures or photographs. Find a face that fits your story and describe it.

As you have seen, heroes need problems to solve. These might be caused by human enemies (antagonists), by their own flaws, or by war, slavery, plague, invasion, or poverty.

A bad situation

In 16th-century Venice, only the eldest daughter of a noble household was allowed to marry. If the family was very rich, the second eldest might also. But in Donna Jo Napoli's *Daughter of Venice*, heroine Donata is a second-born twin, and she reflects on the bind she's in:

Unless I marry, a convent lies ahead for me, too. I'd die in a convent.
Donna Jo Napoli, *Daughter of Venice*

TIPS AND TECHNIQUES

Your villain should be as well thought out as your hero. Don't make villains too obvious. They might even start out as your hero's friend.

GETTING STARTED · SETTING THE SCENE · · · · · · · · CHARACTERS · · · · · · · · VIEWPOINT

24

Enemies everywhere

In *The House of Windjammer* by V. A. Richardson, Adam Windjammer has many enemies, especially the sinister preacher Abner Heems:

> *Abner Heems was just standing there, his hat pulled down low over his eyes ... his shoulders hunched against the cold. The preacher had come stealing to their door as quiet as Death.*
>
> V. A. Richardson, *The House of Windjammer*

Picture of cruelty

In Barbara Smucker's *Runaway to Freedom*, Julilly's main "enemy" is her life of slavery, but she also has a human enemy—the slave overseer, Sims:

> *Mama Sally held Julilly close as they walked outside and joined the field-hand line. The man with the jay-bird voice strode back and forth in front of them. ... His cheeks puffed and jiggled as he walked. Julilly noticed that his fingers puffed, too, over the whip that he flicked in his hand.*
>
> Barbara Smucker, *Runaway to Freedom*

Own worst enemy

In Leon Garfield's *The Empty Sleeve*, Peter Gannet is his own worst enemy. Envy of his twin, Paul, and a burning ambition to run away to sea lead him into a life of dishonesty.

Now it's your turn

Know your villain

Take 10 minutes to brainstorm your hero's human enemy. What does your villain do and what is his or her motivation? Is he or she truly bad or simply a product of the times? Does he or she have weaknesses that will affect the story? Describe what he or she looks like. Draw a picture, too.

DEVELOP A SUPPORTING CAST

The best way to show readers what your hero is really like is to have them interacting with other characters. Minor characters can add drama and complication to the story.

Character sketches

Charles Dickens' books are a good place to learn about creating memorable minor characters. In *Great Expectations*, Pip describes his bullying sister, Mrs. Joe:

> *My sister ... had such a prevailing redness of skin, that I sometimes used to wonder whether it was possible she washed herself with a nutmeg-grater instead of soap.*
> Charles Dickens, *Great Expectations*

Take two

In Geraldine McCaughrean's *Stop the Train*, two mail-order brides step off the Osage stagecoach. From this description, which do you think will be more important to the story?

> *One of the ladies was a slim needle of a woman with plump, pink cheeks, wearing a crushed bonnet and net gloves. The other wore a bright yellow plaid underskirt, her iris-blue overdress caught up behind into a bustle so extravagant that it resembled a bunch of daffodils sprung from a ledge above the sea. A pair of old scarlet riding gloves were tucked into her waistband.*
> Geraldine McCaughrean, *Stop the Train*

GETTING STARTED   SETTING THE SCENE   CHARACTERS   VIEWPOINT

Now it's your turn

Hungry readers

Sum up your story in a single striking sentence, then develop it in two or three short paragraphs. Try to whet your readers' appetites. Show where your story is going without giving away the actual ending.

Think about your theme. In most stories, the general theme is the triumph of good over evil. Historical stories might also tackle the abuse of power, overcoming hardship or persecution, righting a wrong, or getting revenge.

Make a story map

You have a synopsis that says what your story is about. You have a cast of characters and a setting. You know from whose viewpoint you wish to tell the tale. The next useful tool is a story map. Before filmmakers start filming, they map out the plot in a series of sketches or storyboards. This helps them to decide how best to film the story. You can do this for your story. Draw the main episodes in pictures and add a few notes that say what is happening in each scene.

TIPS AND TECHNIQUES

Writing a synopsis can bring unexpected ideas to the surface. If you can't describe your story in a couple of paragraphs, it is too complicated. Simplify it. Keep asking yourself: "Whose story is this and how will I tell it?"

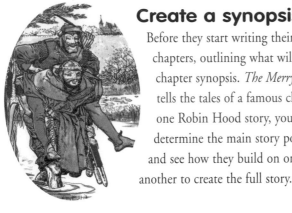

Create a synopsis

Before they start writing their stories, novelists often list all their chapters, outlining what will happen in each one. This is called a chapter synopsis. *The Merry Adventures of Robin Hood* by Howard Pile tells the tales of a famous character in historical fiction. Looking at one Robin Hood story, you can determine the main story points and see how they build on one another to create the full story.

A famous example

Here are storyboard captions for a story in *The Merry Adventures of Robin Hood*:

1. It is the time of Richard I, and the Sheriff of Nottingham sends an outlaw, Guy of Gisbourne, to kill Robin Hood.

2. Robin kills Guy and, disguising himself in Guy's cowl, goes to find the Sheriff.

3. Meanwhile, Little John meets a widow whose sons are to be hanged by the Sheriff.

4. Little John goes in disguise and meets the Sheriff. He agrees to be the hangman.

5. Little John frees the brothers but is captured.

6. As Little John is to be hanged, Robin arrives, dressed as Guy, and says he has killed Robin.

7. For his reward, he asks permission to kill Little John and has him tied to a tree.

8. Robin frees Little John and tells him to pick up the weapons he has hidden in the woods.

9. Robin reveals who he is and draws his bow on the Sheriff.

10. The terrified Sheriff and his men flee for the safety of Nottingham's city gates.

Novels versus short stories

Novels have beginnings, middles, and ends just like short stories, but the stories themselves are more complex. Novels have more details, more character development, and, probably, several subplots. In a larger tale, chapters make the storytelling more manageable. Each one has a beginning, middle, and end, like a mini-story inside the larger one, but it also carries the story forward, adding more mystery and creating more suspense.

Expanding a short story

To make the Robin Hood story into a short novel, you would need to think how each storyboard scene could be expanded to show readers more about the characters, their problems, and the times they lived in. For example, chapter one might start with some historical scene-setting that demonstrates how the Sheriff of Nottingham has gained so much power. If you include a scene with the Sheriff plotting with Guy, this will show readers what kind of villains they are and explain their different reasons for wanting Robin dead. A novel, then, is not a short story made longer, but a short story made deeper.

TIPS AND TECHNIQUES

Don't let a novel's length put you off. It's often easier to write a novel than it is to write a good short story.

Now it's your turn

In a circle

If you are struggling with your story map, try this exercise.

1. Sketch your hero inside a circle in the center of a piece of paper. As you draw, imagine that you are that hero, deciding which way to go. Think about the problems he or she has and what might be done about them.

2. Draw six spokes around your hero circle. Each leads to another circle. Inside each one, sketch a different scene or write it as notes. Each circle will be a course of action that your hero might take or some obstacle in his or her path.

3. Give yourself 20 minutes and write down only your first thoughts.

BAIT THE HOOK

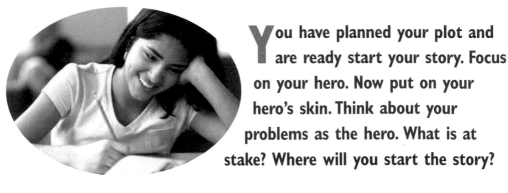

You have planned your plot and are ready start your story. Focus on your hero. Now put on your hero's skin. Think about your problems as the hero. What is at stake? Where will you start the story?

Hooking your readers

Some stories jump right into a dramatic scene, then backtrack shortly afterward to explain things to readers. Others start with a prologue, giving the story's historical context. You could also start with a brief scene set just before a crisis comes. This lets you show the hero's usual life just before a conflict makes it worse—just before a Viking invasion, for example. Your hero must then act or face the consequences.

Fast and furious

Karen Cushman's *Catherine, Called Birdy* is about a teenager in a fury. The date is 1290, and the 14-year-old heroine, Catherine, a minor lord's daughter, has been ordered by her older brother to keep a diary. From the first lines, we are hooked:

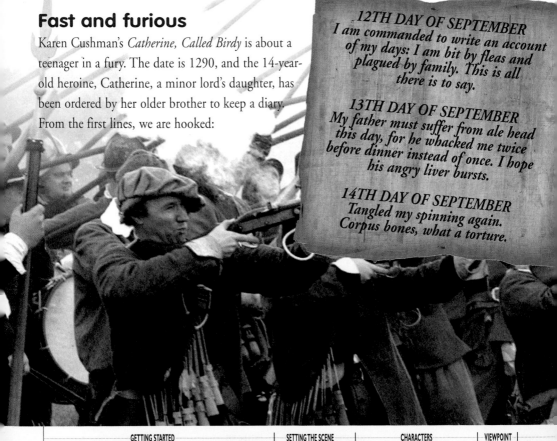

12TH DAY OF SEPTEMBER
I am commanded to write an account of my days: I am bit by fleas and plagued by family. This is all there is to say.

13TH DAY OF SEPTEMBER
My father must suffer from ale head this day, for he whacked me twice before dinner instead of once. I hope his angry liver bursts.

14TH DAY OF SEPTEMBER
Tangled my spinning again. Corpus bones, what a torture.

High tension

V. A. Richardson's *The House of Windjammer* starts with a shipwreck and the loss of a family fortune. From the first lines, we know things will only get worse for the family:

> *They were lost. All aboard the Sirius knew it now. Lucien Windjammer cursed under his breath. The Sirius rode uneasily on the swell, moving through the fog like a ghost ship.*
> V. A. Richardson, *The House of Windjammer*

Bizarre beginnings

In *Daughter of Venice*, Donna Jo Napoli uses names and objects that are common to the location and time period to introduce the setting and make the reader want to learn more.

> *The Canal Grande is busy. That's nothing new to us. From our bedchamber balcony my sisters and I watch the daily activity. Our palazzo stands on the Canal Grande and our rooms are three flights up, so we have a perfect view. But down here in the gondola, with the noise of the boats, and the smell of the sea, and the glare of the sun on the water, not even the thin gauze of my veil can mute the bold lines of this delightful chaos.*
>
> Donna Jo Napoli, *Daughter of Venice*

TIPS AND TECHNIQUES

Study lots of opening sentences. Decide which ones work best and why. Make your own opening mysterious, dramatic, or funny. Write it and rewrite it. Introduce the conflict in the first line, or soon afterward. Send your heroes dramatically on their way.

Stories often falter after an exciting opening, so be sure to build interest and add complication. It is important to find ways to crank up the tension.

Add some action

Keep your characters active at all times—battles, chases, runaway horses, shipwrecks, etc. But be sure the action arises from your characters' plans, and not your need to add excitement. In the excerpt below, see how Crispin gets caught outside and trapped in an alley by men who mean to harm him:

> *Gulping for breath, I halted and spun about, only to find that another man had come up behind me. I flung myself against a wall, even as I struggled to get Bear's dagger out of my pocket. With the two men keeping to either side of me, I was unable to confront them both. But one, I saw, had a large stick in his hand. The other held a knife. "Keep away!" I screamed, finally managing to pull Bear's dagger free from its sheath.*
> Avi, *Crispin: The Cross of Lead*

Character conflict

Supporting characters can add intrigue and suspense. In V. A. Richardson's *The House of Windjammer*, Jade tries to help Adam. However, because she is his enemy's daughter, Adam suspects her at every turn. This puts both of them in danger.

TIPS AND TECHNIQUES

If the middle of your story seems thin, pile on the challenges for your heroes—make their lives miserable. If you run out of ideas, look through your research notes.

False happy endings

These can be useful partway through a story. In *Catherine, Called Birdy*, by Karen Cushman, Birdy's father decides to marry her off to restore the family fortunes. There is a false happy ending when the heroine succeeds in driving away the first suitor. But then her father comes up with another— maintaining the readers' interest and building tension.

Explore your hero's weaknesses

Your hero's weaknesses can add suspense to a tough situation. In Leon Garfield's *The Empty Sleeve*, Peter Gannet lets his ambition lead him into dangerous situations. He soon learns that keys are valuable items and can earn him the money he needs to pay for his passage on a ship. But will his employer find out?

> *For an alarming instant, as he fumbled for the key behind the mirror, he was glared at by his own reflection; and was shocked by how young and frightened he looked. Shakily he got hold of the key and crept down the stairs with it.*
> Leon Garfield, *The Empty Sleeve*

Build stories upon stories

In The Orphan Train Adventures series by Joan Lowery Nixon, the Kelly children are sent on the Orphan Train by their poor, widowed mother to find families who can give them a good life. Each book follows the different Kelly children as they are adopted and brought to their new homes. Frances dresses as a boy to protect her brother. Mike runs away to join the Army. Danny plots to reunite his family. Megan thinks she is cursed by a gypsy. As soon as one book ends, another begins. Will the entire Kelly family ever be settled?

END WITH A BANG

S tories build in suspense until they reach a climax. After this, the heroes' main problems will be solved. If they go back to their old lives, they will have learned something, conquered an enemy, or overcome a weakness.

The climax

In an action story, the climax is likely to be some kind of battle with the main enemy. The enemy might be a person or it might be the learning of a painful truth that sets the hero on a new course and ends the story on a hopeful note.

Counting the cost

Heroes may pay a price for winning in the end. They could lose a friend, a cherished hope, or a valued possession. At the very least, they will be older, and some of their youthful innocence will be lost.

TIPS AND TECHNIQUES

Good endings usually link to the beginning. This reminds readers of how much the hero has changed in the course of the story and how much has happened.

Now it's your turn

Choose your own ending

Read the ending of your favorite historical-fiction book. Decide what you liked about it and what you didn't. Write your own ending. Put it aside and read it later. Do you still think your ending is better?

Endings suggest a new beginning

Most readers like happy endings of some sort, but don't be predictable. In historical fiction, a typical fairy-tale ending won't be believable. Instead, focus on what the hero has gained from his or her experience. The hero may have been hurt but now has a chance to do better and have a good life.

Elizabeth George Speare's ending to *The Sign of the Beaver* suggests more adventures for Matt in the future:

> *Matt thrust his arms into his new jacket ... the cabin glowed, warm and filled with life. ... They would all sit together around the table and bow their heads while his father asked the blessing. Then he would tell them about Attean.*
> Elizabeth George Speare,
> *The Sign of the Beaver*

Bad endings

Bad endings are those that:
- fizzle out if you've run out of ideas
- have historically impossible solutions
- are too good to be true
- are too grim and leave the readers with no hope

MAKE YOUR WORDS WORK

In historical stories, every word must work hard to transport readers back in time. Pick the most telling details to bring the past to life.

Use sharp focus

Choose a few, precise details to create a scene. See how Geraldine McCaughrean describes pioneers stepping off the train in *Stop the Train*:

> *There was a middle-aged man in overalls and a woman's broad-brimmed straw hat. ... There was a widow in black, with a net purse swinging from her wrist, a knitting bag and a goat.*
> Geraldine McCaughrean, *Stop the Train*

Choose your words

Use powerful verbs. Sunlight may "reflect" off a drawn sword. But if it "glances," the verb could suggest a blade slashing in battle.

Now it's your turn

Wise words

Pick a word from a favorite book and, with a friend, take turns to see how many similar words you can come up with. Or pick a new word from the dictionary every day. Find ways to use it—make it part of a poem or brief story.

GETTING STARTED   SETTING THE SCENE   CHARACTERS   VIEWPOINT

Use vivid imagery

In *The Empty Sleeve*, Leon Garfield uses striking similes: A snowstorm is "like a madman made of feathers" and "church steeples were as stiff and white as dead men's fingers." These images foreshadow bad things to come.

Change the rhythm and length of your sentences

Use short, punchy sentences when describing specific actions.

If something scary is going to happen, use longer sentences to build suspense.

Here is Peter Gannet being haunted by the whispers of ghostly apprentices, and that's only the start:

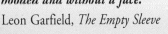
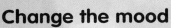

> The whispering stopped. … Then, suddenly, and with a violent rush, the door burst open! Instantly an icy wind rushed in, tore at the candle flame and put it out. Then silence returned. There was someone standing in the doorway … a figure all in black, hooded and without a face.
>
> Leon Garfield, *The Empty Sleeve*

Change the mood

Serious stories need lighter moments to make difficult scenes bearable or to distract readers before something really nasty happens. Humorous stories also need dashes of drama to hold readers' interest.

USE DRAMATIC DIALOGUE

Creating good dialogue is one of the biggest challenges for the historical-story writer. When it's right, it can add color, pace, mood, and suspense to your story.

Let your characters speak

Readers do not want to struggle with writers' attempts at medieval dialogue. When in doubt, opt for plain English that omits current expressions. (Look back at the excerpt from *Catherine, Called Birdy* on page 34. Karen Cushman uses authentic phrases like "corpus bones" and "ale head." But overall the diary is written in understandable English.)

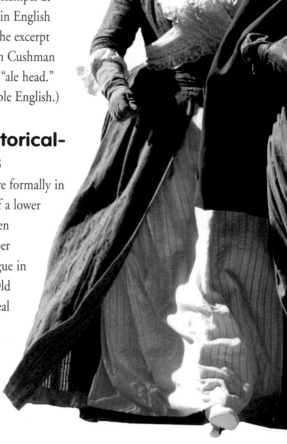

Study other historical-fiction writers

People often spoke more formally in the past, and people of a lower class would have spoken respectfully to the upper classes. Listen to dialogue in historical TV dramas. Old letters can also give us a real sense of the past.

Eavesdrop

Listening to how people around you speak will show you how information flows back and forth between speakers. Notice that people often start mid-sentence or break off without finishing a sentence or thought.

Now it's your turn

Family chat

Spend 10 minutes writing down how your family talks at home. Include all the hesitations and repetitions. Compare your notes to some dialogue in a book. You will see at once that it does not include all the hesitations of natural speech. Fictional dialogue gives an edited impression of real speech.

Following convention

The way dialogue is written follows certain conventions, or rules. It is usual to start a new paragraph for every new speaker. What the speaker says is enclosed in quotation marks, followed by speech tags ("she said," "he said," or "she asked") to show who's speaking.

> *"Grandma says your dad ain't got the sticking power of a monkey on a greased pole."*
>
> *"Excuse me!" retorted Cissy. "I don't know that someone who ain't acquainted with some other person ought to go bandying monkeys...!"*
>
> Geraldine McCaughrean, *Stop the Train*

USE DRAMATIC DIALOGUE

If you need to give readers details of a character's actions or history, it's often quicker and more interesting to do it in a conversation. If characters discuss or argue about something in the past, readers learn lots about them and their history.

Information as conversation

Here's an example from *Carrie's War* by Nina Bawden. Auntie Lou tries to excuse the behavior of her brother, Mr. Evans:

> *"Oh, his bark's worse than his bite. Though he won't stand to be crossed, so don't be too cheeky and mind what he says. I've always minded him—he's so much older, you see."*
>
> Nina Bawden, *Carrie's War*

A sense of doom

In Leon Garfield's *The Empty Sleeve*, Mr. Bagley, the old ship's carpenter, predicts troubles ahead for the Gannet twins:

> *"I done the best I could for your boys, Mr. G," confided the old man, earnestly. "I rigged their vessels under tops'ls only. That way they'll ride out the squalls. ... It's best to be prepared for the worst, Mr. G, for them squalls has got to come. Most of all, for young Peter here. Saturday's child, born on the chime, will surely see ghosts..."*
>
> Leon Garfield, *The Empty Sleeve*

44

GETTING STARTED · · · · · · · · · · · · · · · · · · SETTING THE SCENE · · · · · · · · · · · CHARACTERS · · · · · · · VIEWPOINT

Now it's your turn

The art of communication

Write another descriptive line of dialogue about Mr. Evans based on Auntie Lou's account of him on the previous page. Indicate her feelings about her brother. These are only suggested by what she says, but they are quite important. Think about how a few words of dialogue tell a lot about a character. Once finished, compare your version to the original.

Create tension

Dialogue can be used to create different atmospheres—mysterious, humorous, tragic, or happy. It can be used to build tension and foreshadow dangers ahead. In this excerpt, Adam Windjammer has been waylaid by street boys. Note the sense of menace conjured up by the writer:

"Looks like a rich boy, Wolfie," one said. "Shut your m-mouth, can't you!" the hungry-looking youth stammered... "How many t-times have I told you not to use my name when we're r-robbing?"

"Robbing!" Adam gasped. "But I don't have any money."

"Is that the t-truth of it?" Wolfie said. "Well, we'll be the j-judge of that."

V. A. Richardson,
The House of Windjammer

TIPS AND TECHNIQUES

Avoid idle chatter. If any piece of dialogue doesn't advance your story, cut it out.

USE DRAMATIC DIALOGUE

Good dialogue can reveal what characters are really like. Speech patterns can show social status, education, regional origins, and age, as well as suggesting the historical period.

Class difference

In *The Empty Sleeve*, Leon Garfield uses modern English while showing 18th-century class differences in the ways characters address one another. Here, the young locksmith's apprentice Peter Gannet meets Lord Marriner in the local tavern. The aristocrat calls Peter only by his master's name. In return, Peter uses a formal address and speaks rather nervously, as the stammered "y-yes" hints.

> *"You're Mr. Woodcock's boy, aren't you?" said his lordship, kindly.*
> *"Y-yes, your lordship."*
> *The waiter returned with the port.*
> *"Your health, Mr. Woodcock's boy!"*
>
> Leon Garfield, *The Empty Sleeve*

Regional accents

Used with care, bits of regional speech—turns of phrase and accents—can enrich the characters and make the time and place of the story seem real. The characters in *The Sign of the Beaver* are pioneer settlers in Maine in the 1770s. Elizabeth George Speare makes this apparent through the dialogue and the old-fashioned words, such as "reckon."

> *"Six weeks," his father had said that morning.*
> *"Maybe seven. Hard to reckon exactly."*
>
> Elizabeth George Speare, *The Sign of the Beaver*

GETTING STARTED · SETTING THE SCENE · CHARACTERS · VIEWPOINT

Suggest the past

Caroline Lawrence's The Roman Mysteries series has four very different main characters from Roman times: Flavia, an aristocrat; Jonathan, an outspoken Jewish doctor's son; Nubia, a freed African slave who struggles to speak formal Latin; and Lupus, a mute ex-street boy. The writer adds occasional words or phrases to suggest the period and the characters' backgrounds.

> *"Doctor Mordecai!" gasped Flavia. "You look just like a Roman."*
> *"Behold!" said Nubia. "You have cut your hairs."*
> *With his forefinger, Lupus pretended to shave his own smooth cheeks.*
> *"And shaved off your beard!" agreed Jonathan. "Great Jupiter's eyebrows, father! Why did you do that?"*
>
> Caroline Lawrence,
> The Roman Mysteries

Reveal education

The Seeing Stone is set in 12th-century England, just before the fourth Crusade. The quest for Jerusalem is on everyone's minds. Here, Gatty, a servant girl, shows her lack of education by asking Arthur, a scholarly lord's son, if Jerusalem is farther away than the nearby English city of Chester:

> *"Much, much farther," I said.*
> *"Why?"*
> *"Why's because I want to see where Jesus was born. Instead of Ludlow fair, let's go to Jerusalem."*
> *"Gatty!" I said. "You can't walk to Jerusalem."*
> *"I can and all," said Gatty.*
> *"You can't," I said. "Only a magician could. It's across the sea."*
> *Gatty lowered her head and looked at the ground. "I didn't know that," she said.*
>
> Kevin Crossley-Holland, *The Seeing Stone*

Now it's your turn

Who's who?

Choose two characters from historical fiction who are different from each other in a particular way—perhaps one is richer, more educated, or from a different place or social class. Invent a conversation between them. Think of ways to show their differences—both in their choice of words and in what they say. Take your time; get it just right.

BEAT WRITER'S BLOCK

Sometimes even the best writers can run out of words. This is called writer's block. It can last for days, but regular practice and lots of brainstorming will help. Here are some common causes:

Thinking what you have written is no good

Remember the story executioner—your internal critic that belittles your work? Well, give him the ax. Do some timed brainstorming at once: List the historical figures you'd most like to meet, your time machine's future destinations, how many words mean "old," and so on. Just get yourself writing again.

Thinking everyone else is a better writer

Even experienced writers fall into this trap. But remember, the more you practice, the more you will improve. You could use your skills to write for history magazines. Documenting the past is the biggest story of all!

Case study

The poet Samuel Taylor Coleridge had one of the first known cases of writer's block. In 1804 he wrote: "Yesterday was my Birth Day. So completely has a whole year passed, with scarcely the fruits of a month—O Sorrow and Shame. I have done nothing!"

Now it's your turn

Mystery time travel

In your next writing practice, imagine you are traveling in your time machine once more. It stops. The door opens. Step outside. Search for clues that tell you where you've landed. Are you pleased or petrified? Pour out your thoughts for 10 minutes.

No ideas

Thinking you have no ideas is a common block, but as a history lover, you will never run short of material. There are centuries' worth of stories waiting to be told. Visit your local museum, a national museum, or a favorite historic place. Go out and search for a story.

Rejection or external criticism

No one enjoys rejection or criticism, but it is an important part of learning to be a writer. If you invite someone to share your stories, be prepared for some negative comments. They may be more useful than flattery. See them as a reason to improve and rewrite your story if it really needs it.

If you are stuck mid-story, you may not have done enough planning. Do you know what your hero really wants? Ask yourself if your plot has left him or her stranded.

Ways to stir your imagination

"What if?" is a good question to ask if your story isn't quite clear. What if the hero is really a noble person's son but doesn't realize it? This is what happens in Charles Dickens' famous book *Oliver Twist*, where the boy is seemingly condemned to life in the workhouse.

Character forming

If you still don't know your hero well enough to work out his or her story, try this exercise. Write the heading "My Hero" on a sheet of paper. Divide the left margin into 10 squares, with the following headings in each one: looks; wears; lives in; feels; owns; is good at; is bad at; his or her weakness is; his or her friends are; and his or her enemies are. For each category, take five minutes to write five thoughts. When you have finished, you will know 50 things about your hero.

Keep a diary

If you keep a journal, you should never stop writing. When you visit museums and other historic places, be sure to record all your thoughts and impressions. These could provide valuable research ideas. Make sure you read what you have written regularly.

Brainstorm with friends

Writing can be a lonely business. If your key character isn't coming to life, brainstorm with friends. Sit in a circle. Start by telling them a brief outline of your character's situation and who he or she is. Then let everyone ask you questions or make suggestions about what will happen next. It may help you to solve a serious plot problem.

Breaking down resistance

If you really are stuck with your writing, try telling someone else's story. Retell a local legend or use the *Robin Hood* synopsis on page 32 to write your own version of that story. The main thing is to finish it. Completing a piece of storytelling like this will spur you on with your own tales. Prove that you can finish something.

TIPS AND TECHNIQUES

Staring at a blank page waiting for inspiration to strike will only give you a headache and make you feel bad about yourself. Brainstorm a list. Write something. Something can always be improved. Nothing can't.

TAKE THE NEXT STEP

Completing your first story is a wonderful achievement. You have started to master your writer's craft and probably learned a lot about yourself, too. But now, you must seek out another quest. Put your first story away in your desk drawer and start a new tale.

THE END

Another story?

If you did a lot of research for your first story, the chances are you will already have enough material to write another. Perhaps, while you were writing, some other character's story drew your interest. See if there's an angle for another story.

How about a sequel to your first story?

Is there more to tell about the characters you have already created? Can you write a sequel that says what happens next? Celia Rees continued one of her stories when she wrote *Sorceress* as the sequel to *Witch Child*. Perhaps your hero is ready for another adventure, or maybe your novel features a minor character who deserves his or her own story.

What about a trilogy?

A trilogy usually covers one main story, split over three volumes. V. A. Richardson's *The House of Windjammer* and Kevin Crossley-Holland's Arthur books are trilogies. The hero's main problems are revealed in the first book, expanded in the second, and resolved in the third.

Or a quartet?

Joan Lowery Nixon wrote four books in The Orphan Train Adventures. The writer was inspired by tragic real-life events in 19th-century America when poor East Coast families were forced to send their children to the West on the orphan trains, hoping they would be adopted by pioneering families who could give them a better life.

Search the archives

Keep looking for stories: Visit museums, look through history books, learn about a specific invention, read the diary of a real historical figure, or nag a grandparent for more family stories. Joan Lowery Nixon got the idea for her stories this way. She says she wanted to "bring history and fiction together in an exciting, adventurous time and place, to tell the stories of those who could have traveled west on the orphan train."

Storytelling is a special skill, and success will not come overnight. Most well-known writers worked for years before publishing, and few authors make a living from writing. It is something people do for reasons other than money and fame.

So why do writers write?

- They write because they must.

- They write to tell a story that must be told.

- They write because they believe that nothing is more important than stories.

- They write because it's the thing they most want to do.

Celia Rees

Celia Rees (right), author of *Witch Child*, realized that the skills that condemned a woman to death in 17th-century Europe were valued among American Indians. What if a girl could move between those two societies? She said:

Writing a book, any book, is like taking a journey. You know the starting point, and (more or less) where you are heading, but you have no way of knowing exactly what is going to happen in between.

Rosemary Sutcliff

Rosemary Sutcliff, author of *Tristan and Iseult,* was born in England but spent her early life in Malta. She wrote 46 novels for young people. She was a sickly child and was home-schooled, and it was during this time that her mother read her the Celtic and Saxon legends that were to fire her love of history.

Elaine Marie Alphin

Elaine Marie Alphin (right), author of *Ghost Soldier*, wanted to be a paleontologist when she grew up, but writing became her great love. She says she writes "to make sense of my life, and out of the world around me. I write to explore new ideas."

Karen Cushman

Karen Cushman (below), author of *Catherine, Called Birdy*, didn't start writing books professionally until she was 50 years old. She especially liked the Middle Ages because big changes were happening in the way people looked and behaved, and how they thought about their own identity. These have connections with issues that young people face today. She says:

> *My ideas come from reading and listening and living; they come from making mistakes and figuring things out. Ideas come from wondering a lot—such as what would happen if ... ? And then what would happen next?*

After your story has been resting in your desk for a month, take it out and read through it. You will be able to see your work with fresh eyes and spot strengths and flaws easily.

Edit your work

Reading your work aloud will help you to simplify rambling sentences and correct dialogue that doesn't flow. Cut out all unnecessary adjectives and adverbs, and extra words like "very" and "really." This will instantly make your writing crisper. Once you have cut down the number of words, decide how well the story works. Does it have a satisfying end? Has your hero resolved the conflict in the best possible way? When your story is as good as can be, write it out again or type it up on a computer. This is your manuscript.

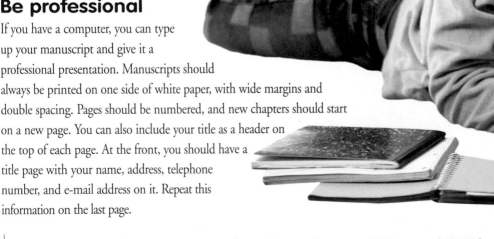

Think of an exciting title

It is important to think of a good title—something intriguing and eye-catching. Think about some titles you know and like.

Be professional

If you have a computer, you can type up your manuscript and give it a professional presentation. Manuscripts should always be printed on one side of white paper, with wide margins and double spacing. Pages should be numbered, and new chapters should start on a new page. You can also include your title as a header on the top of each page. At the front, you should have a title page with your name, address, telephone number, and e-mail address on it. Repeat this information on the last page.

Make your own book

If your school has its own computer lab, why not use it to publish your own story or to make a story anthology (collection) with your friends. A computer will let you choose your own font (print style) or justify the text (making even margins like a professionally printed page). When you have typed and saved your story to a file, you can edit it quickly with the spelling and grammar checker, or move sections of your story around using the cut-and-paste tool, which saves a lot of rewriting. Having your story on a computer file also means you can print a copy whenever you need one, or revise the whole story if you want to.

Design a cover

Once your story is in good shape, you can print it out and use the computer to design the cover. A graphics program will let you scan and print your own artwork, or download ready-made graphics. Or you could use your own digital photographs and learn how to manipulate them on-screen to produce some highly original images. You can use yourself or friends as models for your story's heroes.

TIPS AND TECHNIQUES

Whether you write your story on a computer or by hand, always make a copy before you give it to others to read. Otherwise, if they lose it, you will have lost all your precious work.

REACH YOUR AUDIENCE

The next step is to find an audience for your historical fiction, whether it's a novel or a short story. Family members or classmates may be receptive. Or you may want to share your work through a Web site, magazine, or publisher.

Some places to publish your story

There are several magazines and a number of writing Web sites that accept stories and novel chapters from young writers. Some give writing advice. Several run regular competitions. Each site has its own rules about submitting work, so make sure you read them carefully before you send in a story. You can also:

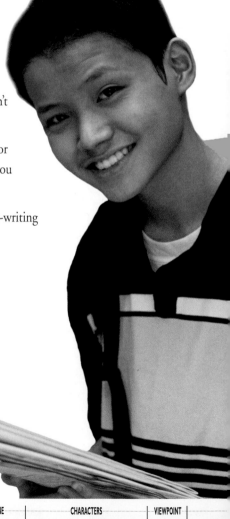

• Send stories to your school's magazine. If your school doesn't have a magazine, start your own with like-minded friends.

• Keep your eyes peeled when reading your local newspaper or magazines. They might be running writing competitions you could enter.

• Check with local museums and colleges. Some run creative-writing workshops during school holidays.

Writing clubs

Starting a writing club or workshop group and exchanging stories is a great way of getting your historical-fiction story out there. It will also get you used to criticism from others, which will prove invaluable in learning how to write. Your local library might be kind enough to provide a space for such a club.

Finding a book publisher

Study the market and find out which publishers are most likely to publish historical fiction. Addresses of publishers and information about whether they accept submissions can be found in writers' handbooks at your local library. Bear in mind that manuscripts that haven't been asked for or paid for by a publisher—unsolicited submissions—are rarely published. Secure any submission with a staple or paperclip and always enclose a short letter (explaining what you have sent) and a stamped, self-addressed envelope for the story's return.

Writer's tip

If your story is rejected by an editor, see it as a chance to make it better. Try again, and remember that having your work published is wonderful but it is not the only thing. Being able to make up a story is a gift, so why not give yours to someone you love? Read it to a younger brother or sister. Tell it to your grandmother. Find your audience.

Some final words

All good stories show us the truth about ourselves, even when they are about times long past. Historical fiction helps us to understand the past in different ways. But whether past or present, the best stories always explore the good and bad things that make us human. They show us new possibilities.

GLOSSARY

anachronism—something that is placed in the wrong historical time (such as a telescope in the hands of a Roman soldier)

analogy—a comparison that shows the resemblance between things in order to explain something clearly

antagonist—principal character in opposition to the protagonist or hero in fiction

chapter synopsis—an outline that describes briefly what happens in each chapter

cliffhanger—ending a chapter or scene of a story at a nail-biting moment

dramatic irony—when the reader knows something the characters don't

editing—removing all unnecessary words from your story, correcting errors, and rewriting the text until the story is the best it can be

editor—the person at a publishing house who finds new books to publish and advises authors on how to improve their stories by telling them what needs to be added or cut

first-person viewpoint—a viewpoint that allows a single character to tell the story as if he or she had written it; readers feel as if that character is talking directly to them; for example: "It was July when I left for Timbuktu. Just the thought of going back there made my heart sing."

foreshadowing—dropping hints of coming events or dangers that are essential to the outcome of the story

genre—a particular type of fiction, such as fantasy, historical, realistic, mystery, adventure, or science fiction

manuscript—your story when it is written down, either typed or by hand

metaphor—calling a man "a mouse" is a metaphor, a word picture; from it we learn in one word that the man is timid or weak, not that he is actually a mouse

motivation—the reason why a character does something

narrative—the telling of a story

omniscient viewpoint—an all-seeing narrator that sees all the characters and tells readers how they are acting and feeling

plot—the sequence of events that drive a story forward; the problems that the hero must resolve

point of view (POV)—the eyes through which a story is told

primary source—the term historians use to describe firsthand accounts written in the historical period they are studying, such as letters, diaries, or official documents like wills and marriage licenses

protagonist—the main character in a play or book

publisher—a person or company who pays for an author's manuscript to be printed as a book and who distributes and sells that book

sequel—a story that carries an existing one forward

simile—saying something is like something else, a word picture, such as "clouds like frayed lace"

synopsis—a short summary that describes what a story is about and introduces the main characters

theme—the main idea behind a story, such as overcoming a weakness, the importance of friendship, or good versus evil; a story can have more than one theme

third-person viewpoint—a viewpoint that describes the events of the story through a single character's eyes, such as "Jem's heart leapt in his throat. He'd been dreading this moment for months."

unsolicited submission—a manuscript that is sent to a publisher without being requested; these submissions usually end up in the "slush pile," where they may wait a long time to be read

writer's block—when writers think they can no longer write or have used up all their ideas

Visit your local libraries and make friends with the librarians. They can direct you to useful sources of information, including magazines that publish young people's short fiction. You can learn your craft and read great stories at the same time. Librarians will also know if any published authors are scheduled to speak in your area.

Many authors visit schools and offer writing workshops. Ask your teacher to invite a favorite author to speak at your school.

On the Web

For more information on this topic, use FactHound.
1. Go to *www.facthound.com*
2. Type in this book ID: 0756516404
3. Click on the *Fetch It* button.
FactHound will find the best Web sites for you.

Read more historical fiction

Alphin, Elaine Marie. *Ghost Soldier*. New York: Henry Holt, 2001.

Bawden, Nina. *Carrie's War*. Philadelphia: Lippincott, 1973.

Crossley-Holland, Kevin. *The Seeing Stone*. New York: Arthur A. Levine Books, 2001.

Curtis, Christopher Paul. *The Watsons Go to Burmingham*. New York: Delacorte Press, 1995.

Cushman, Karen. *Catherine, Called Birdy*. New York: Clarion Books, 1994.

Donnelly, Jennifer. *A Northern Light*. San Diego: Harcourt, Inc., 2003.

Erdrich, Louise. *The Birchbark House*. New York: Hyperion Books for Children, 1999.

Giff, Patricia Reilly. *Lily's Crossing*. New York: Delacorte Press, 1997.

Lowry, Lois. *Number the Stars*. Boston: Houghton Mifflin Co., 1989.

McCaughrean, Geraldine. *Stop the Train*. New York: HarperCollins, 2003.

Napoli, Donna Jo. *Daughter of Venice*. New York: Delacorte Press, 2002.

Park, Linda Sue. *A Single Shard*. New York: Clarion Books, 2001.

Pfitsch, Patricia Curtis. *Riding the Flume*. New York: Simon & Schuster Books for Young Readers, 2002.

Rees, Celia. *Witch Child*. Cambridge, Mass.: Candlewick Press, 2001.

Salisbury, Graham. *Under the Blood-Red Sun*. New York: Delacorte Press, 1994.

Smucker, Barbara Claassen. *Runaway to Freedom: A Story of the Underground Railway*. New York: Harper & Row, 1978.

Taylor, Mildred D. *Roll of Thunder, Hear My Cry*. New York: Dial Press, 1976.

Walsh, Jill Paton. *A Parcel of Patterns*. New York: Farrar, Straus, and Giroux, 1983.

Westall, Robert. *The Machine Gunners*. New York: Greenwillow Books, 1976.

Whelan, Gloria. *Homeless Bird*. New York: HarperCollins, 2000.

Read all the Write Your Own books:

Write Your Own Adventure Story
ISBN: 0-7565-1638-2

Write Your Own Fantasy Story
ISBN: 0-7565-1639-0

Write Your Own Historical Fiction Story
ISBN: 0-7565-1640-4

Write Your Own Mystery Story
ISBN: 0-7565-1641-2

Write Your Own Realistic Fiction Story
ISBN: 0-7565-1642-0

Write Your Own Science Fiction Story
ISBN: 0-7565-1643-9

INDEX

Picture Credits: Art Archive: 8b, 32t, 35t, 46-47 all. Alamy: 40l. Corbis RF: 1, 4, 13b, 14t, 18-19c, 40-41c, 41 all, 49r, 50t, 50b, 54t &c, 58-59 all. Creatas: 6t, 8t, 12t, 23t, 29br, 30t, 42t, 43 all, 48t, 56-57 all. Dickens House Museum: 10t, 16t. Getty images: 44-45c, 45t, 51t, 52-53c, 53t. Rex Features: 5 & 24, 6-7c, 8-9c, 9r, 11b, 18t, 20t, 22t, 22-23c, 26-27c, 28t, 28-29c, 30-31c, 32-33c, 33t, 34-35b, 36-37 all, 38-39 all, 42b, 42-43c, 44t, 50-51c, 54-55c, 55t & b, 60t. Werner Forman Archive: 7r, 11t, 12b, 13t, 14-15c, 16-17 all, 20-21c & r, 24t, 24c, 25t, 26t, 30b, 34t, 40b, 48b, 49t.

Every effort has been made to contact copyright holders of any material reproduced in this book. Any omissions will be rectified in subsequent printings if notice is given to the publishers.

MISSION UNSTOPPABLE

10 INTERACTIVE BIBLE STUDIES FOR
SMALL GROUPS AND INDIVIDUALS

BRYSON SMITH

matthiasmedia

SYDNEY · YOUNGSTOWN

Matthias Media
(St Matthias Press Ltd ACN 067 558 365)
Email: info@matthiasmedia.com.au
Internet: www.matthiasmedia.com.au
Please visit our website for current postal and telephone contact information.

Matthias Media (USA)
Email: sales@matthiasmedia.com
Internet: www.matthiasmedia.com
Please visit our website for current postal and telephone contact information.

ISBN 978 1 921896 43 9

Cover design and typesetting by Matthias Media.
Series concept design by Lankshear Design.

›› CONTENTS

›› HOW TO MAKE THE MOST OF THESE STUDIES

1. What is an Interactive Bible Study?

Interactive Bible Studies are a bit like a guided tour of a famous city. They take you through a particular part of the Bible, helping you to know where to start, pointing out things along the way, suggesting avenues for further exploration, and making sure that you know how to get home. Like any good tour, the real purpose is to allow you to go exploring for yourself—to dive in, have a good look around, and discover for yourself the riches that God's word has in store.

In other words, these studies aim to provide stimulation and input and point you in the right direction, while leaving you to do plenty of the exploration and discovery yourself.

We hope that these studies will stimulate lots of 'interaction'—interaction with the Bible, with the things we've written, with your own current thoughts and attitudes, with other people as you discuss them, and with God as you talk to him about it all.

2. The format

The studies contain five main components:
- sections of text that introduce, inform, summarize and challenge
- numbered questions that help you examine the passage and think through its meaning
- sidebars that provide extra bits of background or optional extra study ideas, especially regarding other relevant parts of the Bible
- 'Implications' sections that help you think about what this passage means for you and your life today
- suggestions for thanksgiving and prayer as you close.

3. How to use these studies on your own

- Before you begin, pray that God would open your eyes to what he is saying in the Bible, and give you the spiritual strength to do something about it.
- Work through the study, reading the text, answering the questions about the Bible passage, and exploring the sidebars as you have time.
- Resist the temptation to skip over the 'Implications' and 'Give thanks and pray' sections at the end. It is important that we not only hear and understand God's word, but also respond to it. These closing sections help us do that.
- Take what opportunities you can to talk to others about what you've learnt.

4. How to use these studies in a small group

- Much of the above applies to group study as well. The studies are suitable for structured Bible study or cell groups, as well as for more informal pairs and triplets. Get together with a friend or friends and work through them at your own pace; use them as the basis for regular Bible study with your spouse. You don't need the formal structure of a 'group' to gain maximum benefit.

- For small groups, it is *very useful* if group members can work through the study themselves *before* the group meets. The group discussion can take place comfortably in an hour (depending on how side-tracked you get!) if all the members have done some work in advance.
- The role of the group leader is to direct the course of the discussion and to try to draw the threads together at the end. This will mean a little extra preparation—underlining the sections of text to emphasize and read out loud, working out which questions are worth concentrating on, and being sure of the main thrust of the study. Leaders will also probably want to work out approximately how long they'd like to spend on each part.
- If your group members usually don't work through the study in advance, it's extra important that the leader prepares which parts to concentrate on, and which parts to glide past more quickly. In particular, the leader will need to select which of the 'Implications' to focus on.
- We haven't included an 'answer guide' to the questions in the studies. This is a deliberate move. We want to give you a guided tour of the Bible, not a lecture. There is more than enough in the text we have written and the questions we have asked to point you in what we think is the right direction. The rest is up to you.

5. Bible translation

We quote from and refer to the English Standard Version, which we recommend. There should not generally be any problems, however, if you are using a different translation. (Nevertheless, it might be useful to have an ESV on hand in case of any confusion.)

6. Before you begin

We recommend that before you start study 1, you take the time to read right through Acts in one sitting. This will give you a feel for the direction and purpose of the whole book and help you greatly in looking at each passage in its context.

THE ACTS OF THE ~~APOSTLES~~ RISEN CHRIST

[ACTS 1:1–2:41]

1. What do you already know about the book of Acts?

written by Luke
mostly about declaring the gospel

O N SATURDAY 2 SEPTEMBER 2000, the Sydney 2000 Olympic torch relay came through the town in which I live. The Olympic torch had originally been lit by the sun's rays at a special ceremony in Olympia, Greece. When the flame finally arrived in Australia it stayed for 100 days, being carried by 11,000 torchbearers through more than 1,000 towns. The torch visited every state and territory, and it journeyed within one hour's drive of 85% of the Australian population. Apart from the traditional runners, the torch travelled via train, plane, bicycle, stock horse, camel, tram, road train, row boat, Chinese dragon boat, canoe, ferry, solar-powered vehicle, surf boat and the Royal Flying Doctor Service. And on a wet, overcast Saturday morning, the torch came through my town.

What was interesting was the massive excitement the Olympic torch relay generated, especially amongst the torchbearers themselves. One of them told me, "It's such a privilege to be involved in an event this big. I may never do anything else, but I'll be able to tell my children that at least their mum carried the Olympic flame." Another commented, "Going to work each day, doing the washing, watching the TV, it's all so small. But to carry the Olympic flame even for a little while, it's so much bigger than anything else I've done. I wanted to be part of the relay because I wanted to be part of something bigger than my life."

Do you sometimes feel like that? The alarm goes off in the morning, you roll out of bed for another day and it's the same old routine. Everything seems so mundane and small scale. Do you sometimes feel that it would be nice to be caught up in something a bit more spectacular than what your life usually seems to be?

The book of Acts is a wonderful book, because it helps us to see that when we are followers of Jesus we actually are caught up in something much bigger than ourselves. As Christians, we are caught up in a worldwide movement that makes the Olympic torch relay pale into insignificance. We are involved in the passing on of a message that has been transforming people's lives in every single country on the face of this earth for thousands of years. What's the key to seeing this? Realizing that Acts is a book all about Jesus Christ.

Read Luke 1:1-4 and Acts 1:1-3.

2. In what ways are the books of Luke and Acts similar? In what ways are they different?

> both addressed to Theophilus
> Luke -why he's writing this
> Acts- gets right into it

3. What is the significance of the word 'began' in Acts 1:1?

> it's about Jesus' story but not all of it bc
> it's not over

Read Acts 1:4–8.

4. It would seem that the apostles are going to have an important role in what Jesus will continue to do and teach. What does Jesus want the disciples to do, and why?

   go out and witness so that they can be fruitful

5. What signs are there that Jesus' plans are different from what the disciples expected (vv. 6-8)?

   The Father has the authority + it is not for the disciples to know his plan

6. The apostles were people like Peter, James, John... What do you know of their track record with Jesus up until then? How surprising is Jesus' mission for them?

   They have all fallen short so its a testament to Jesus' forgiveness

Read Acts 1:9–26.

7. What characteristics must Judas' replacement have? Why are they important?

   They must witness

Optional question

Skim back over chapter 1, and list as many examples as you can of Jesus being the one in charge and controlling all the action.

Welcome to the sequel

ACTS IS THE SECOND VOLUME OF A two-volume work. The first volume is the Gospel of Luke. It's unfortunate that our English Bibles usually place John's Gospel between the two, as Luke and Acts belong together. They are two volumes that focus on the same person: Jesus Christ. Luke's Gospel is about what Jesus *began* to do and teach. Acts is about what he *continues* to do and teach.

It will be helpful to bear this in mind during these studies, for it will stop us misapplying the text. For example, in the book of Acts, Luke describes many unusual and extraordinary events, and there is a danger of thinking that these events should also happen to us. We need to realize that Luke may be recording something simply because that's what happened then, and not necessarily because it's what should happen for us now. We take this for granted at certain points. For example, in Acts 1 we have just read of Jesus telling his disciples to wait in Jerusalem. Does that mean we are all to fly to Jerusalem and wait for a word from the Lord as well? Of course not—we realize that, in this respect, the apostles are unique. They are specific people in a specific place at a special point of history.

Realizing that Acts is essentially about Jesus will help us to avoid that danger. As we read through Acts, we must keep asking ourselves the question: what are we discovering about the risen Jesus Christ?

One of the big lessons in chapter 1 is that the ongoing work of the risen Christ involves the spreading of his gospel to the ends of the earth (1:8). This is a vitally important work because of what we discover about Jesus in the next chapter.

Read Acts 2:1-13.

8. What happened to the apostles when they were first filled with the Holy Spirit? How does this fit with Jesus' mission briefing back in 1:8?

They spoke in tongues. They will recieve power

Read Acts 2:14-21.

9. According to verse 17, the filling of the apostles with the Holy Spirit reflects that the "last days" have now commenced. According to verse 20, what do these last days precede?

Jesus' Second coming

creation   fall   redemption   (new creation)

10. The "day of the Lord" is a reference to the final judgement when God will punish all sin. What is it necessary to do during these last days preceding the day of the Lord (v. 21)?

be saved , repent

Read Acts 2:22-36.

In these verses, Peter tells the crowd some crucial things about Jesus. Let's tease out the main points of his speech.

11. According to verses 22-24, what did men do to Jesus? What did God do?

men crucified +killed Jesus
God resurrected Jesus

12. According to verse 27, what did the Old Testament predict about God's coming king? In the light of your answer to the previous question, what does this tell us about Jesus?

Jesus would be resurrected

13. According to verse 33, where is Jesus now and what has he done?

Seated at the right hand of The Father

14. According to verse 34, what else did the Old Testament predict about God's coming king? What does this tell us about Jesus?

He comes from David's line

15. Peter has been drawing some parallels between Jesus and the Christ predicted in the Old Testament. Verse 36 now comes as Peter's punchline. Try rewriting it in your own words.

Let everyone know that Jesus who was crucified is Lord and Messiah with assurance.

Read Acts 2:37–41.

16. What is the crowd's reaction? What does Peter say they should do, and why?

they were "cut to the heart" and wanted to be saved. Peter tells them to repent + be baptized to recieve the Holy Spirit.

Apostles behaving strangely

ON THAT FIRST PENTECOST FEAST after Jesus' resurrection, the apostles are certainly doing some strange things: even speaking in different languages that they're not meant to know! However, the key issue is not whether we should do what the apostles did—the key issue is what we discover about the risen Christ. In fact, we discover something of enormous importance about Jesus.

The apostle Peter explains that the apostles are acting strangely so as to signal that "the last days" have arrived (2:17). In other words, the clock is now running and God's judgement is coming. The "great and magnificent" day of the Lord is approaching (2:20)—the day when God will judge and punish all sin. The good news is that in these last days people can escape God's judgement by calling on the name of the Lord (2:21). The bad news for the people of

Jerusalem, however, is that the Lord they're meant to be calling on is actually the man they killed a couple of months back (2:36)!

Jesus has shown himself to be the Lord by rising from the dead. Peter says that God predicted it (2:25-31) and he himself has seen the risen Christ (2:32). This Jesus whom they crucified is therefore both Lord and Christ. They need to call on him for help before it is too late!

This emphasizes the importance of Jesus' mission plan (1:8). No wonder it's important for the news of Jesus to be spread in Jerusalem, Judea, Samaria and to the ends of the earth. Jesus' death and resurrection have ushered in the last days. Now is the time to call on Jesus for help, before it is too late. Now is the time to warn and plead with others, before it is too late.

» Implications

(Choose one or more of the following to think about further or to discuss in your group.)

- In what ways are we different from the apostles? In what ways are we similar?

- In what ways are we different from the crowd in Acts 2? In what ways are we similar?

- Where do we fit into Jesus' mission plan of 1:8? What difference should this mission plan make to us?

- Is there any one truth about the risen Christ that has especially struck you from this study? How should it shape the way you live?

» Give thanks and pray

- Thank God for his long-laid plan to send Jesus so that everyone who calls upon his name will be saved.
- Praise God for revealing this plan to humanity through his word in the Old and New Testaments, through his filling Spirit, and through the signs and wonders performed by the Son.
- Ask God to help you fulfil your role as a Christian in these last days by spreading the news of Jesus' death and resurrection.

APOSTLES BEHAVING BRAVELY

[ACTS 3-5]

Every now and then, our governments have what we call an amnesty—a time when the government says that people who are doing something wrong can stop doing it, own up to it, and they won't be punished. In Australia, back in 1997, there was a gun buyback amnesty. People had until a certain date to hand in certain types of guns without punishment. They'd get off scotfree. But if they refused the amnesty and they got caught with the guns later… then they'd be in trouble.

In our last study we discovered that the death and resurrection of Jesus have ushered in an amnesty with God. The "last days" have started. This is the time before God's final judgement, in which we can move from being in trouble with God to being right with him. More than that, we now have the opportunity of being on *close personal terms* with God. We can have his Spirit. It's just a matter of taking advantage of God's amnesty by submitting and trusting the risen Christ as both Lord and Saviour.

It's a very exciting offer from God. Let's see how the people in Jerusalem responded to it.

A remarkable miracle

Read Acts 3.

1. Who does this miracle involve and where does it take place?

2. What does the man do after being healed? Note especially where he goes.

The scene that follows this miracle is very similar to that which followed the events of Pentecost in Acts 2. Peter uses an extraordinary event as an opportunity to witness about Jesus.

3. Compare Peter's speech here in Acts 3 with the one he made in Acts 2. Note in particular:

- What truths about Jesus does Peter repeat?

- What response does Peter call on the crowd to make?

A remarkable confrontation

Read Acts 4:1–22.

4. Why do Peter and John get arrested?

5. How do Peter and John react to their arrest?

6. What new things do we discover about the risen Christ from this confrontation?

A remarkable prayer

Read Acts 4:23–31.

7. What do the believers pray? In what way is this surprising?

Psalm 2

After Peter and John's release, the believers quote Psalm 2 in their prayers. Psalm 2 describes the kings of this world lined up against God's holy king. God's king laughs at the puniness of their opposition, and warns them to submit before it's too late. (If you have time, why not read the psalm?) How are the apostles 'living out' the message of Psalm 2?

A picture of the gospel

THE HEALING OF THE CRIPPLED beggar receives more attention than any other healing in the book of Acts. That's deliberate, because this healing provides us with a picture of what happens when someone calls on the name of Jesus for help. The chapter opens with the beggar outside the temple, ceremonially unclean. Following his healing, the beggar enters the temple, praising God. It's a wonderful picture of what Jesus can achieve in these last days. A person who was unacceptable is made acceptable. Now he can enter the intimacy of God's presence for the first time in his life—and all by the power of Jesus' name. It's a miracle that symbolizes the gospel.

That's certainly what Peter wants the crowds to understand. He takes the opportunity to explain again the importance of Jesus. In a speech very similar to his Pentecost speech, Peter urges the Jews to turn their lives over to Jesus before it's too late (3:19-20).

Peter and John's conviction of the importance of Jesus also shines out in their confrontation with the Jewish leaders. This confrontation must have been very scary for them. They are in the very spot where Jesus had stood not long before. They are standing trial in the room in which Jesus probably stood trial, before the men who condemned Jesus to death, arrested for much the same reasons. The authorities don't like the claims about Jesus. Peter and John must have been thinking that it was their turn now to face death. This is what makes their speech so remarkable. It is a speech of courage, born out of the conviction that it is vitally important for people to hear about Jesus (4:8-12).

As we shall see, it will not be the last time Peter makes such a speech.

Read Acts 4:32–5:11.

8. In what ways were the believers caring for one another?

9. What was Ananias and Sapphira's sin?

10. In what ways does this incident show that the church is very precious to the risen Christ? How does this explain the "great fear" that seized the church (5:11)?

Read Acts 5:12-42.

Think about the overall pattern of events in these verses. They show a basic similarity: the apostles perform miracles; the gospel is preached; the apostles are arrested and threatened; the apostles boldly keep preaching.

11. What is *different* between Acts 5:12-42 and Acts 3-4? Consider:

- the reason for the opposition

- the number of people involved

- the intensity of the opposition

Gamaliel's caution

What is Gamaliel's argument (5:33-39)? What do you think of it?

12. What does Peter mean in verse 29?

13. What do we learn about Jesus from Peter's speech?

Opposition to the risen Christ

WE'VE COVERED A BIG SECTION OF Acts in this study, but it's helpful to do so. Reading big sections at a time can open our eyes to patterns and themes within the book. In particular, we have seen the theme developing of opposition to the ongoing work of the risen Christ. Both inside and outside the church, we have seen sinful people seeking to hinder and exploit the work of Christ. This opposition to Jesus will reach its ugliest in our next study.

Against this background of increasing opposition, it's also important to notice the need to have an appropriate fear of the risen Christ. After Peter and John's first arrest, the believers were spurred on by the truths of Psalm 2, a psalm which warned the rulers of the earth to "serve the LORD with fear" (Ps 2:11). For this reason, the apostles continue to testify about Jesus. They desire to revere and obey God, not man.

Fear of the risen Christ is also part of the incident of Ananias and Sapphira. Ananias and Sapphira's punishment for treating the church with contempt reflects the value with which the risen Christ holds his church. Christ takes it very personally when his church is mistreated (see also Acts 9:4 for this close personal link between Jesus and his church). For this reason, "great fear came upon the whole church" (5:11).

Such references to fearing the risen Christ are appropriate. Jesus' resurrection has shown him to be the Lord and Christ of the world. Jesus holds power and authority beyond our imagination. The idea of disobeying Christ should therefore terrify us. The thought of ignoring or refusing Christ, or seeking to manipulate him, should fill us with dread. If it doesn't, then we have no idea who we're dealing with. As Jesus himself explained to his disciples:

> "I tell you, my friends, do not fear those who kill the body, and after that have nothing more that they can do. But I will warn you whom to fear: fear him who, after he has killed, has authority to cast into hell. Yes, I tell you, fear him!" (Luke 12:4-5)

» Implications

(Choose one or more of the following to think about further or to discuss in your group.)

- So far we have seen the work of the risen Christ opposed because of theological reasons (4:2) as well as crass jealousy (5:17). In your experience, what are other reasons that Christianity is criticized and opposed?

- "Peter and John are superheroes of the faith. It's easy for them to be so brave. I'm just a normal person. I can't be expected to be as bold as them." What do you think about a comment like that?

- "We must obey God rather than men" (5:29). When do you find this especially hard? What are some specific, practical ways we can help each other in this matter?

- How should a reverent fear of the risen Christ influence:
  - how we handle temptation?

  - the way we treat other Christians?

  - our attitude to church?

  - our prayer and Bible reading?

  - facing persecution?

  - our evangelism?

» Give thanks and pray

- Praise God for being a God of justice who frees the innocent and judges those who harm his people. There is no people or power who can successfully stand against him.
- Thank God for giving boldness to his servants through his Holy Spirit.
- Ask God for forgiveness for the times you have sinned against and mistreated his body, the church.

THE VOICE OF THE MARTYR

[ACTS 6-7]

1. Discuss some of the ways in which the ongoing work of the risen Christ has been opposed in Acts so far.

WE DON'T TEND TO LIKE MONO-polies in our world. That's because a monopoly takes control away from us. When we don't have a choice and we *have* to deal with a certain person or organization, it puts us at a disadvantage.

Over the last two studies, one of the things that has become crystal clear is that Jesus has a monopoly over us. As the risen Christ of God, Jesus is the appointed king over all the earth. We cannot escape his dominance or his superiority over us. Furthermore, because of Jesus' unequalled authority and power, he is the only person who can help us escape God's judgement. Salvation is found in no-one else. There is no other name under heaven by which we can be saved.

All this means that Jesus has a complete and utter monopoly over us. He is the one we must obey in this life, and he is how we gain salvation for the next life. This is exactly what rubs so many people the wrong way. We don't like monopolies in anything, especially religion! It is inevitable, therefore, that the monopoly of Jesus produces conflict. We've already noticed this conflict in our last study. But it's about to get a lot worse!

Read Acts 6:1–7.

2. What is the source of the tension amongst the believers?

3. What solution is reached? Do you think this is a good solution? Why or why not?

4. In what way has Jesus' mission plan (1:8) shaped the church's dealing with this problem (6:2)?

Division, diversion and delegation

OUR SECTION OPENS WITH A SERIous division within the church. Grecian Jews (those Jews who'd been brought up with Greek education and culture) are complaining that the more conservative Hebraic Jews are getting better treatment than they are. The complaint is no small thing. The words used in 6:1 have echoes of the murmuring, bickering and whining of Israel in the wilderness after the exodus (Exod 16:7; Num 14:27). Out of this unease, another threat also develops—not only divisiveness but diversion (Acts 6:2). The danger is that the apostles will be pressured to stop doing the best thing for the sake of doing a good thing. They have been commissioned by God to testify about Christ (1:8), but now the danger is that they'll be distracted from this task (6:2).

The solution is delegation. Seven are chosen to make sure that all the widows are being equally cared for. Enter Stephen, a dear brother in Christ on whom the text now focuses.

Read Acts 6:8–15.

5. Who are the people opposing Stephen?

6. What specific charges are made against Stephen, and why do you think these charges are so serious?

7. In what ways is this opposition to Stephen similar to, and different from, the opposition that Peter and John faced in Acts 3–4 and Acts 5?

Stephen, the law and the temple

THE SCENE HAS SUDDENLY CHANGED from internal tensions to external danger, as Stephen is hauled before the Sanhedrin to give a defence of his actions. It is important to notice the specific charges that are brought against Stephen: that he speaks "against this holy place and the law" (6:13). The 'holy place' is a reference to the Jerusalem temple, and the 'law' is a reference to the Old Testament law. It is with these accusations in mind that Stephen now launches into his defence.

Read Acts 7.

8. Why do you think Stephen recounts so much of the Old Testament in his speech?

9. Stephen has been accused of being against the temple. What does Stephen say about the temple in verses 44-50? In what way is this a defence against the accusations?

10. Stephen has been accused of being against Moses. What does Stephen say about Moses in verses 35-39? In what way is this a defence against the accusations?

11. What is it in Stephen's speech that most annoys the Sanhedrin?

12. What do you think Stephen means in verse 56?

Saul

In 7:58-8:1 we are introduced to a young man named Saul. What impressions do you get of him? (Hold onto this thought for our next study.)

13. What finally happens to Stephen? How do you feel about that?

The church's first martyr

THE ESCALATING HOSTILITY THAT WE have noted in Acts has finally exploded. The blood of the church's first martyr now runs in the streets of Jerusalem. It is a tragic and brutal moment in the history of the early church. Yet even through the tragedy, we discover important things about the ongoing work of the risen Christ. Two particular truths deserve mention.

a) The divisiveness of Christ

In Luke's first volume, Jesus said to his disciples:

> "Do you think that I have come to give peace on earth? No, I tell you, but rather division. For from now on in one house there will be five divided, three against two and two against three. They will be divided, father against son and son against father, mother against daughter and daughter against mother, mother-in-law against her daughter-in-law and daughter-in-law against mother-in-law." (Luke 12:51-53)

Jesus predicted precisely what we've been seeing in Acts. The circumstances and people involved may differ, but the same basic pattern keeps reappearing. The risen Christ brings division.

b) The continuity of Christ

Stephen's speech is the longest speech in Acts. Clearly Luke thought that what Stephen said is important. We can get a bit lost in such a long speech, but the main point is simple enough. Stephen is keen to show that the coming of Jesus is in complete continuity with the Old Testament.

The specific charges made against Stephen were that he opposed the temple and the Old Testament law. In his lengthy defence, Stephen argues that it is the *Sanhedrin* who have got things all out of proportion. With regards to the temple, Stephen points out that God worked unhindered without a temple for many years (7:2-43), and that when a temple did finally come along it was at David's, and not God's, initiative (7:46); nor was God in a hurry to build it, since it was delayed until Solomon's reign (7:47). Indeed, when it finally was built, God declared the temple inadequate and only a symbol of his dwelling (7:48-50). The implication is clear. The Sanhedrin think that Stephen has it wrong about the temple, but Stephen argues that *they* are the ones who need to go back and read their Old Testament! The temple is not nearly as significant as they think.

The other main accusation against Stephen was that he was anti-Moses and the Law. It's in defending this charge that Stephen most angers the Sanhedrin.

Stephen recounts the events of the Old Testament, and points out that it is the Sanhedrin who come from a long line of ancestors who reject God (e.g. 7:9, 25-27, 34-35, 39-43). Just in case the speech has been a little too subtle for the Sanhedrin, Stephen closes off by saying:

> "You stiff-necked people, uncircumcised in heart and ears, you always resist the Holy Spirit. As your fathers did, so do you. Which of the prophets did your fathers not persecute? And they killed those who announced beforehand the coming of the Righteous One, whom you have now betrayed and murdered, you who received the law as delivered by angels and did not keep it." (Acts 7:51-53)

Stephen's point is now pretty obvious. The Sanhedrin have accused him of being against the temple and God's law; however it is they themselves who are wrong about the temple, and disobedient to the workings of God. Far from being in contradiction to the Old Testament, Jesus the risen Christ is the *climax* of the Old Testament.

» Implications

(Choose one or more of the following to think about further or to discuss in your group.)

- In Acts 6:1-2, the disciples are in danger of being diverted from the task to which God had called them. In what ways are we susceptible to the same danger? Can you think of 'good' things which can divert us from the 'best' things in following the risen Christ?

- In what ways do you see the divisiveness of Christ in your life?

- "The God of the Old Testament is one of wrath and judgement, but the God of the New Testament is one of grace and love." What do you think about this comment? How do you think Stephen would respond to it?

- In what way is Stephen a good example for us to follow?

» Give thanks and pray

- Praise God for the many different ways that we can serve and care for each other. Praise him for the Christians around you and the particular gifts he's given them.
- Thank God for the privilege of reading Stephen's explanation of how God worked through the history of the Israelites.
- Ask for endurance and perseverance for those who are experiencing real hardship because of their faith.
- Ask God to give you the boldness of Stephen.

THE UNSTOPPABLE KING

[ACTS 8:1-9:31]

1. Imagine you are a Christian during the time of Acts. How would you be feeling by the end of Acts 7?

THE SONG 'CANDLE IN THE WIND' by Elton John is *the* biggest-selling song worldwide since charts began. Elton John originally wrote the song about Marilyn Monroe. It describes her life as a candle in the wind—a life that was a brief flickering flame, which shone brightly for a while, but all too soon was gone. What really made sales of the song soar, however, was when Elton John adapted and performed it at Princess Diana's funeral. Hers was another life that many people felt shone brightly for

a while, but all too soon was gone.

If you had to pick a person in Acts who fitted the song 'Candle in the Wind', it would have to be Stephen, the Christian brother we examined in our previous study. Everything that we really know about Stephen is confined to those two chapters of Acts. Stephen appears, shines brilliantly for a brief moment, and then he's gone. A candle in the wind.

However, the section of Acts which we have now reached shows that Stephen's life was also a flame in a much bigger fire. The fire of the risen Christ's Spirit was sweeping through the hearts and minds of men, women and children. It was, and is, a fire which cannot be contained—a fire which burns even to this day. We, too, have the privilege of being a flame in this fire.

Read Acts 8:1–3.

2. What were the negative results of Stephen's death?

3. Why do you think the apostles stayed in Jerusalem?

4. What do we discover about Saul in these verses? What impression do you have of this man? (Keep your answer in mind for the second half of this study.)

Read Acts 8:4–25.

5. What positive thing resulted from the death of Stephen? In particular, how are verses 1 and 4 especially significant, given what Jesus had said in 1:8?

6. What did Simon get wrong? In what way is he similar to Ananias and Sapphira?

Optional: read Acts 8:26–40.

- To whom does Philip explain the gospel? What things do we know about this person? Why do you think Luke singles out this event to tell us?

7. Why do you think the apostles sent Peter and John to Samaria?

- Why do you think we are told that "the Spirit of the Lord carried Philip away" (v. 39)?

8. Why do you think the Holy Spirit had not come upon any of the people prior to the arrival of Peter and John?

Onwards and outwards!

WAY BACK IN ACTS 1:8, WE DISCOV-ered that the risen Christ's mission plan was for the gospel to be preached in Jerusalem, Judea, Samaria and to the end of the world. Up until now, Acts has been focusing on the Jerusalem stage of the plan. Now in chapter 8, Jesus' plan moves into its next phase: the gospel spreads from Jerusalem into Judea and Samaria (8:1).

The significance of this moment in Acts is highlighted in two ways. Firstly, the apostles in Jerusalem send Peter and John to confirm this development (8:14). Secondly, Luke records the unprecedented way in which the giving of the Holy Spirit is delayed until the apostles arrive in Samaria. This is very unusual, and serves to emphasize that the gospel has now crossed a most significant barrier. It is as if the risen Christ wants to show, beyond doubt, that the step into Samaria has his approval. He waits until the apostles are there to see for themselves that even the Samaritans (mixed-race Jews) are now receiving the Holy Spirit.

This section powerfully reflects Christ's determination for his gospel to be spread. Even in the midst of persecution, his church still grows. The scattering of the Christians because of the persecution only has the effect of spreading the gospel even more! Christ really is unstoppable; a truth driven home in the next chapter.

Read Acts 9:1–2.

9. How would you describe Saul in these verses (and using what we already know of Saul from earlier in Acts)?

Read Acts 9:3–9.

10. How would you describe Saul now?

Read Acts 9:10–25.

11. What do you think of Ananias' fear?

12. God has a job for Saul. Describe it in your own words.

13. How would you describe Saul now?

Read Acts 9:26–31.

14. How would you describe Saul now?

15. In what ways is verse 31 a fitting summary for the whole of Acts so far?

From persecutor to apostle

IT IS A REFLECTION OF THE authority of the risen Christ that he can humble someone as intimidating as Saul. Indeed, it's not enough that Saul just becomes a Christian; Christ now uniquely charges Saul to spread the very gospel which he had been trying to stamp out. It is a beautiful irony that the man who hated Christians because they weren't Jewish enough is now going to be instrumental in spreading the gospel to the non-Jews (9:15-16)!

Here is the power of the risen Christ. The master executioner is humbled, and led into Damascus like a prisoner of war. Saul, the persecutor of the church, has now become Paul, the apostle to the Gentiles. The man who was determined to stop Christ's ongoing work is now going to be used by Christ so as to achieve his ongoing work. We are seeing that nothing can stop the risen Christ! No wonder the church lived in fear of the Lord (9:31).

» Implications

(Choose one or more of the following to think about further or to discuss in your group.)

- In what ways do we see the sovereignty of God operating in Acts 8-9? How is this an encouragement to us?

- Rejoicing and joy are often associated with conversions in Acts (e.g. 8:8, 39). Often in our experience this initial joy seems to subside with time. Why do you think that is, and how can we help each other prevent this from happening?

- With the persecution that rises up after Stephen's death, God took a bad situation and used it for his own purposes. Can you think of instances when God has done that in your own life?

- "If God can forgive Saul, he can forgive anyone!" Do you think that's true? In what ways do we sometimes limit God's grace?

- Paul would often write about his conversion in his letters. Read the following passages, and in each case consider what valuable lessons Paul draws from his conversion.

  - 1 Corinthians 15:3-11

  - Galatians 1:11-24

» Give thanks and pray

- Praise God for keeping his word: the news of Jesus has been spreading for 2000 years, and he has given many the boldness to witness for Christ.
- Thank God that opposition against the gospel cannot stand, and thank him for turning evil into a testimony to his power.
- Pray that those who are persecuting followers of "the Way" (9:1-2) in our present time would have the scales removed from their eyes, that they may then serve the Lord.

FAVOURITISM-FREE ZONE

[ACTS 10–12]

Life can be full of surprises. Liliana Parodi of Genoa, Italy, went to her favourite restaurant for some pasta. While eating her meal, she bit down on something hard that wedged painfully in her teeth. Complaining loudly, she left. The next morning a dentist extracted the object—an uncut diamond worth $3000. Now there's a meal with a surprise!

In this study we'll discover how Peter had a vision of another meal with a surprise.

Read Acts 10:1–23.

1. What do we discover about Cornelius in these verses?

2. Why do you think Cornelius needed a vision to encourage him to invite Peter?

---

3. Describe in your own words the content of Peter's vision. (For the artistic, try drawing it.)

4. What does Peter mean when he says that some animals are "unclean" (v. 14)?

Read Acts 10:24–48.

5. What lesson does Peter say he learned from his vision of the foods? How does he put that lesson into practice?

6. Peter tells Cornelius about Jesus. The climax of the speech is in verse 43. Why does the word 'everyone' have special significance in verse 43? (See also how Peter starts his speech in verses 34-35.)

7. How do the Gentiles respond to Peter's message? How do the Jews who are there respond?

Read Acts 11:1-18.

8. Why is Peter criticized by the believers in Jerusalem? What is his response?

Optional question

In describing these events, Luke repeats a lot of details from the previous chapter. Why do you think he does that?

Read Acts 11:19–30.

9. What type of people are turning to Jesus in these verses? How is this similar to the events involving Cornelius?

10. Why do you think the believers in Jerusalem sent Barnabas to Antioch? Why is Barnabas a particularly good person to send? (Compare 4:36 and 11:20.)

11. Why is it natural that Barnabas would contact Saul? (See 9:26-29.)

Look who's being saved now!

WE HAVE JUST READ ONE OF the biggest moments in the book of Acts. Back in Acts 1:8, the risen Christ said that he wanted the news about him to be spread throughout Jerusalem, all Judea, Samaria and to the end of the earth. Previously, we have seen the gospel move through the first three areas. Like ripples spreading out on a lake, the gospel has been spreading out, converting Jews in Jerusalem, Jews in all Judea, even half-caste Jews in Samaria. But now, here in Acts 10, the gospel has broken through an enormous racial barrier on its way to the end of the earth: Gentiles are now becoming Christians! Moreover, it is *obvious* that they are becoming Christians, because they're speaking in tongues just like the apostles did at Pentecost. It really is like Pentecost all over again. Here is *the* moment when God's Spirit pours out into the hearts of the Gentiles.

Sometimes it is suggested that as Christians, we should all have the experience that Cornelius and his friends have here. However, Cornelius' conversion is a very special moment in the book of Acts, which makes it unwise to draw general conclusions from this chapter. The tone of the passage is that this is a remarkable, unique event. We, now, are *not* the first Gentiles receiving the Jewish Messiah's Holy Spirit for the first time. Acts 10 is an unrepeatable turning point in salvation history. The news of Jesus has now gone to the Gentiles on its way to the end of the earth.

Furthermore, as we noted in study 1, the key issue throughout Acts is not whether we should do and experience what the early believers did. The key issue is: what do we discover about the risen Christ here? We discover that he does not show favouritism. His mission is for *all* peoples to be saved. Indeed, the next chapter shows us yet again how determined the risen Christ is about his mission!

Read Acts 12:1-19.

12. How do the details of Peter's imprisonment (vv. 4, 6) make his escape all the more dramatic?

13. If the believers were praying for Peter (v. 5), why were they so surprised when he escaped?

Read Acts 12:20-25.

14. Compare the attitude of Herod (vv. 21-23) with that of Peter (10:25-26).

15. Which king is victorious—Herod or the risen Christ? (Don't be afraid to say the obvious—it's not a trick question!)

When two kings go to war

THE FLOW OF IDEAS IN ACTS 10-12 IS very similar to chapters 8-9. In both instances we have seen the risen Christ's gospel cross a significant barrier (to the Samaritans in Acts 8, and to the Gentiles in Acts 10). In both cases, there is also an immediate display of Christ's immeasurable authority (the conversion of Saul in Acts 9 and the death of Herod in Acts 12). Acts is driving home the lesson that the spread of the gospel cannot be stopped, because behind it lies an unstoppable Saviour.

» Implications

(Choose one or more of the following to think about further or to discuss in your group.)

- Peter realizes that "God shows no partiality" (10:34). In what ways do we sometimes show favouritism in:

  - our evangelism?

- our church relationships?

- So far in Acts, we have seen that the risen Christ is powerfully committed to saving all peoples. To what extent do you share this desire? How can we encourage each other to share Jesus' priorities?

- Barnabas has appeared in Acts a few times now. Skim back over the following verses and see what type of person he is: 4:36-37, 9:26-28, 11:22-26, 12:25. In what ways is Barnabas a good example for us?

>> Give thanks and pray

- Praise God that he does not show partiality in who he saves, but instead forgives the sins of all who believe in Jesus.
- Thank God for Jesus the victorious king who is far more worthy of worship than any earthly ruler or hero.
- Ask that you would be willing to have your assumptions challenged and changed by God's word, just as the early Jewish Christians were.

ROAD TRIP

[ACTS 13:1-15:35]

1. What have been the main events so far in Acts? Why are these important?

W E LIVE IN A WORLD THAT LOVES to travel. It is estimated that three million passports are checked at airports and border crossings around the world every day.[1] To give you an idea of just how many that is: if all the passports checked in just one day were piled on top of each other, they would form a stack nine kilometres high, making it taller than Mount Everest!

Maybe it's because we're so used to travelling that we easily miss the profound thing that happens in the next section of Acts. For the first time, the news about Jesus starts to travel in a whole new way.

Re-read Acts 11:19–30 and then read Acts 13:1–3.

2. What impression do you have of the church at Antioch?

Read Acts 13:4–12.

3. Trace Paul and Barnabas' route on the map provided.

4. Why do you think they headed for Cyprus first? (Have a look back at 4:36 and 11:19-20.)

Read Acts 13:13–52.

5. Continue to trace Paul and Barnabas' route on the map.

6. What do we discover from **Paul's speech** about Jesus' place in God's plans (vv. 23, 32-33)?

Paul's speech

Luke gives much space to recording Paul's speech at Pisidian Antioch. There are probably two main reasons for this.

1) This is Paul's first recorded speech in Acts, and so Luke is keen to show us that Paul preached the same gospel as the other apostles. It is, again, ironic that Paul's speech is very similar to Stephen's in its emphasis on Jesus fulfilling the Old Testament. It's a reflection of the authority of Christ that Paul is spreading the same message as the man he once helped to execute!

2) Luke probably also records this speech in detail to show that Paul's expulsion from the city was totally unjustified (13:50). As we will see, Paul's blamelessness will develop into a major theme.

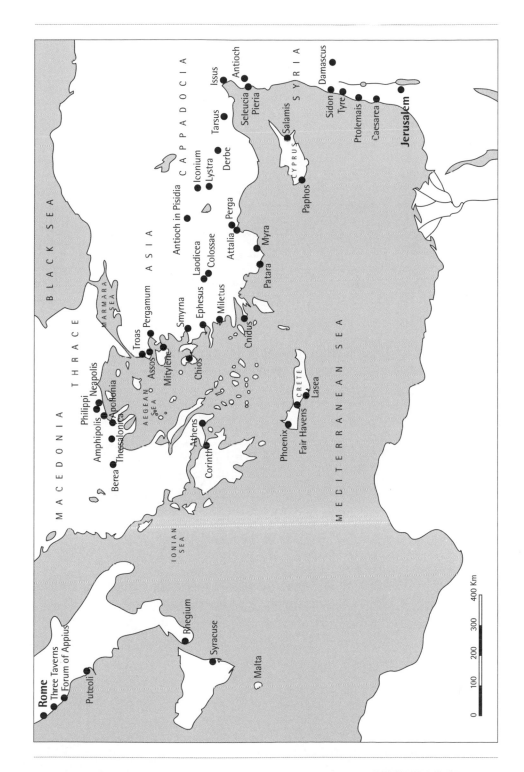

Optional question

In his speech, Paul quotes several sections from the Old Testament. What is his point in each case?

- Psalm 2, quoted in verse 33

- Isaiah 55, quoted in verse 34

- Psalm 16, quoted in verse 35

- Habakkuk 1, quoted in verse 41

- Isaiah 49, quoted in verse 47

7. How do the following groups respond to Paul's message?

- the Jews

- the Gentiles

8. How do these reactions fit with God's plans for Paul? (Compare 9:15.)

Read Acts 14.

9. Continue to trace Paul and Barnabas' route on the map.

10. In what ways are their experiences in Pisidian Antioch repeated in other towns?

11. What impression do you have of Paul from his behaviour in verses 19-20?

12. Skim back over Paul and Barnabas' trip, and list the different ways we have seen Jesus to be in charge.

Victory parade

AFTER BEING AWAY FOR ABOUT TWO years and travelling around 2000 km, Paul and Barnabas are back home in Antioch. Their first missionary journey is now finished. In many ways, the trip has been a victory parade for the risen Christ. In city after city, Paul and Barnabas proclaimed the greatness of Jesus and the victory that he has had over death. Along the way, the risen Christ has also displayed his power and authority many times. As sorcerers are struck down with blindness, as cripples are healed, as Paul receives strength to go on even after a massive beating, and as the hearts of both Jews and Gentiles are stirred and lives are changed, the risen Christ broadcasts his greatness—reflecting the truth that he really is at the centre of everything that God has ever planned (13:32-33).

As we will see, though, not everyone is impressed with this emphasis on Jesus.

Read Acts 15:1–35.

13. What problem comes to the fore after Paul and Barnabas' trip (13:39; 15:1, 5)? Do you think this is a serious issue? Why/why not?

14. What does Peter say regarding the necessity of Gentiles to be circumcised (vv. 6-11)?

Optional question

The Council at Jerusalem, having made it very clear that Gentiles are not saved by being circumcised but are saved by the grace of God through the forgiveness of sins, went on to urge Gentile believers to abstain from food sacrificed to idols, from blood, from meat of strangled animals and from sexual immorality. This is most likely out of pastoral concern, so that there might be no unnecessary barriers to fellowship between Gentile and Jewish Christians (v. 21). Do you think this was a good idea? Why/why not?

15. What does James say regarding the necessity of Gentiles to be circumcised (vv. 13-21)?

Christian crisis talks

PAUL AND BARNABAS' MISSIONARY trip seems to have the effect of bringing into focus a smouldering tension within the early church—a tension between Jewish and Gentile Christians.

From the outset, the church at Antioch was made up of many Gentile believers (11:20-21), and now they are proactively sending missionaries to Gentile cities in which many more Gentiles are becoming Christians. This has sparked a debate over just how Jewish these Gentile believers have to be. Some believers from the Pharisee party are saying that Gentile Christians need to be circumcised—that is, they need to become Jews in order to be fully Christian. Crisis talks are called in Jerusalem, and from these a very clear message is sounded: "We believe that we will be saved through the grace of the Lord Jesus, just as they will" (15:11).

This shines the spotlight on a wonderful truth about the risen Christ. It is a truth already sounded in other parts of Acts: "*Everyone* who calls upon the name of the Lord shall be saved" (2:21); and "by him *everyone* who believes is freed from everything from which you could not be freed by the law of Moses" (13:38-39).

» Implications

(Choose one or more of the following to think about further or to discuss in your group.)

- It is not mentioned in Acts, but it is at about this time that Paul wrote his letter to the Galatians. It seems that the men mentioned in 15:1 (or at least people like them) had followed Paul and Barnabas around on their trip, telling the new believers that they should be circumcised. When Paul heard about this, he wrote to the Galatians. Read Galatians 2:11-21. What new facts does this add to the events of Acts 15?

- In what ways does Galatians 2:15-16 provide a good summary of the issues raised at the Council in Jerusalem?

- If we're saved by what Jesus does and not by what we do, does it matter how we behave? Why can't we sin all the more?

- Do you think it is arrogant to be confident about going to heaven? Why/why not?

» Give thanks and pray

- Praise God for the great successes of Paul and Barnabas' long trip, and for the boldness and strength he gave them in the face of persecution.
- Thank God for the wisdom and insight he gave to those considering the issue of the law and the Gentile believers at the assembly in Jerusalem, and for the way he continues to guide us in decision-making today.
- Ask God to help you use your freedoms wisely, and not be tempted to impose extra burdens on others for the appearance of outward holiness.

Endnote
1. Russell Ash, *The World In One Day*, Dorling Kindersley, London, 1997, p. 29.

POSTCARDS FROM PAUL

[ACTS 16:11–18:22]

1. Try arranging the following events in chronological order (without sneaking a look in your Bible): Ananias' death, Stephen's death, the church at Antioch formed, the council at Jerusalem meets, disciples receive the Holy Spirit, Cornelius receives the Holy Spirit, Peter and John heal a crippled beggar, Saul's conversion, Paul and Barnabas' journey through Galatia.

It's always nice to receive postcards from friends on holidays. It may not be as good as *being* on holidays, but it's nevertheless nice to catch up on friends' news and to hear what things they've been doing. The section of Acts in this study is a bit like a series of postcards from the apostle Paul. In these chapters, Paul is on another journey, to tell the gospel to more people. Along the way, we get to see some of the most significant things which happen to him. We're going to focus on events in Philippi, Thessalonica, Athens and Corinth. In each case, we discover something exciting about the risen Christ.

Postcard from Philippi

Read Acts 16:11–40.

2. In every other city Paul has visited so far, he has started his preaching at the synagogue. How is Philippi different? What does this suggest about Philippi?

3. List all the different people who are converted at Philippi (assume that the slave girl is one). What does this suggest about the diversity of the Philippian church?

4. Why do you think Paul demands that the magistrates "come themselves and take us out" (v. 37)?

Postcard from Thessalonica

Read Acts 17:1–15.

5. Trace Paul and Timothy's route on the map on page 51.

6. What words are used to describe the manner in which Paul shared the gospel at Thessalonica (vv. 2-4)? What do these words tell us about the nature of the gospel?

7. What range of reactions does the gospel receive in both Thessalonica and Berea? How reasonable do you think each of these reactions are?

8. How long did Paul spend in Thessalonica? Given the events of his stay, what do you think might be the dangers and challenges for the new church there?

9. Why do you think we are specifically told that in both cities prominent women and God-fearing Greeks believed (vv. 4, 12)?

Postcard from Athens

Read Acts 17:16-34.

10. What was it about seeing idols that would have made Paul feel so distressed (v. 16)?

Optional question

Most of Luke's description of Paul's visit to Athens is taken up with Paul's speech. Have a go at writing a summary of Paul's speech by writing the following verses in your own words:

• verse 24

▶

• verse 26

11. What does Paul's distress cause him to do? What reactions does he receive?

• verse 27

• verse 29

• verse 30

• verse 31

Postcard from Corinth

Read Acts 18:1-22.

12. Continue to trace Paul and Timothy's route on the map on page 51.

13. It is during Paul's time in Corinth that Silas and Timothy rejoin him with good news from Thessalonica. The encouragement Paul receives from this news (1 Thess 3:6-10) seems to be the trigger for Paul to move to full-time gospel preaching. How do the Jews react to Paul's preaching? Why shouldn't this surprise us?

14. Why do you think the risen Christ chose this specific moment to comfort Paul with words of protection in verses 9-10?

15. What do you think of Gallio's attitude towards the Jews' complaints about Paul?

» Implications

(Choose one or more of the following to think about further or to discuss in your group.)

• Paul was to later write to the Philippian church:

> So if there is any encouragement in Christ, any comfort from love, any participation in the Spirit, any affection and sympathy, complete my joy by being of the same mind, having the same love, being in full accord and of one mind. (Phil 2:1-2)

Why would these words have been particularly appropriate, given what we have discovered of this church? What lessons are there for us in these words?

• "Christianity is just a blind leap of faith." What do you think of this statement, and why?

- Some people suggest that Paul's speech at Athens is a good model for our own evangelism. What do you think?

- As Paul wandered around Athens he was distressed at all their idols. If Paul was to wander through your home, what idols might he see there? How distressed are you about them?

- Do you think God's promise to Paul in 18:9-10 has any implications for us?

» Give thanks and pray

- Praise God that he chooses all kinds of people to belong to his church, from the poor to the powerful. Praise him for his ability to look at people without prejudice or assumption (something we often fail to do).
- Thank God for the way he provides comfort when we need it, from miraculous deliverance to encouragement from his word or a friend.
- Ask God to help you to evangelize faithfully wherever he has placed you—in work, study, childraising or full-time ministry.

ON THE ROAD AGAIN

[ACTS 18:23–21:16]

1. Paul has now been involved in two missionary journeys. What have you found to be the most memorable moment of them so far?

IN OUR LAST STUDY, WE FOLLOWED Paul on his second missionary journey. In particular, we looked at events in Philippi, Thessalonica, Athens and Corinth. In this study, we follow Paul on his third missionary journey, and this time our focus will be on the city of Ephesus. The Holy Spirit had directed Paul away from Ephesus in the early stages of his previous trip (16:6), and so he only briefly visited the city during his return to Antioch (18:19-22). Paul, however, seems very keen to spend time in Ephesus on his third missionary journey.

Ephesus was a very significant city. Standing on the main eastern route from Rome, it was the greatest commercial city of Asia Minor. It enjoyed political importance as a free Greek city, and it also prided itself on the cult of the goddess Artemis. The Temple of Artemis was one of the seven wonders of the ancient world. Given the amount of time which Paul spent in Ephesus, he probably considered the city of great strategic importance for the gospel. But what sort of reception would Paul and the gospel receive there?

Read Acts 18:23–19:7.

2. What has happened in Ephesus since Paul's last (very brief) visit in 18:19-21? How might these events explain the incomplete knowledge of the disciples whom Paul meets in 19:1-2?

3. Luke is tantalizingly brief concerning the inadequacies of Apollos and the disciples whom Paul meets in 19:2. The emphasis is not so much on the details of their incompleteness, but that it is only with Christ that completeness comes. How does this illustrate what Paul has said earlier in Pisidian Antioch (13:32-33)?

Read Acts 19:8–22.

4. In what ways do we see the power and authority of the risen Christ in this section?

Read Acts 19:23–41.

5. What are the motives behind the opposition to the gospel in these verses? Can you think of any other examples in Acts where we have seen this?

6. In Demetrius' speech (vv. 24-27), what does he get right and what does he get wrong?

7. How does the town clerk's speech to the crowd (vv. 35-41) highlight the unreasonableness of the crowd's behaviour?

The place has changed but...

ARE YOU STARTING TO FEEL AS IF you've been here before? Paul's ministry in Ephesus follows the same pattern as it did in so many other towns and cities. The gospel is preached, many people believe, and the word of the Lord spreads widely, but for various reasons opposition also grows. What is distinctive in Ephesus, however, is the emphasis on the extraordinary miracles done through Paul. Perhaps in a city which was so well known for the goddess Artemis (19:35), Luke is keen to show the supremacy and power of the risen Christ. How pathetic it is that the "great goddess Artemis" needs to be protected by a rag-tag bunch of rioters—most of whom don't even know why they're there (19:32)! Meanwhile the risen Christ is healing the sick and removing evil spirits—with the use of a handkerchief. There really is no comparison. No wonder "the name of the Lord Jesus was extolled" (19:17). The risen Christ is in a league of his own. Although he didn't mean them to, Demetrius' words ring very true indeed: "gods made with hands are not gods" (19:26).

Read Acts 20:1–16.

8. Luke now runs through a great many destinations, giving each only a fleeting mention. Trace the route on the map on page 51.

Luke seems keen to move the story along to Paul's arrival in Jerusalem. But before that, there is one more significant interaction between Paul and the church at Ephesus.

Read Acts 20:17–38.

9. How does Paul describe his ministry in Ephesus?

10. Why do you think Paul is so keen to explain the blamelessness of his ministry?

11. What does Paul say the future holds for him? What is motivating Paul to press on with his plans?

12. What does Paul say the future holds for the Ephesian church? How should they behave because of this?

Read Acts 21:1–16.

13. What things happen in these verses to confirm Paul's words that "the Holy Spirit testifies to me in every city that imprisonment and afflictions await me" (20:23)?

Fond farewells and worrying warnings

WE LEAVE THIS STUDY WITH SOME concern about what is still to come. Paul is courageously making his way to Jerusalem, despite every indication that trials await him there. Like Christ himself in Luke's first volume, Paul is determined to travel to Jerusalem and complete the task set before him by God. In many ways, Paul is living out Jesus' words:

> "If anyone would come after me, let him deny himself and take up his cross daily and follow me. For whoever would save his life will lose it, but whoever loses his life for my sake will save it. For what does it profit a man if he gains the whole world and loses or forfeits himself? For whoever is ashamed of me and of my words, of him will the Son of Man be ashamed when he comes in his glory and the glory of the Father and of the holy angels." (Luke 9:23-26)

» Implications

(Choose one or more of the following to think about further or to discuss in your group.)

- In commenting about Priscilla and Aquila's dealings with Apollos (18:26), FF Bruce writes: "How much better it is to give such private help to a teacher whose understanding of his subject is deficient than to correct or denounce him publicly!"[1] Do you agree with this comment? Do you think there is ever a place for public correction and denouncement?

- In what ways is Paul a good example for us to follow in this section?

- Do you think the future dangers that Paul foresaw for Ephesus are also dangers for us? What practical things can we do to "pay careful attention" to ourselves (20:28)?

- In the book of Revelation, Jesus has this to say to the Ephesian church:

  "To the angel of the church in Ephesus write: 'The words of him who holds the seven stars in his right hand, who walks among the seven golden lampstands.
  "'I know your works, your toil and your patient endurance, and how you cannot bear with those who are evil, but have tested those who call themselves apostles and are not, and found them to be false. I know

you are enduring patiently and bearing up for my name's sake, and you have not grown weary. But I have this against you, that you have abandoned the love you had at first. Remember therefore from where you have fallen; repent, and do the works you did at first. If not, I will come to you and remove your lampstand from its place, unless you repent. Yet this you have: you hate the works of the Nicolaitans, which I also hate. He who has an ear, let him hear what the Spirit says to the churches. To the one who conquers I will grant to eat of the tree of life, which is in the paradise of God."' (Rev 2:1-7)

How do the events of Acts help us better appreciate the background to Jesus' words? Do you think Jesus' words have applications for us? If so, what?

» Give thanks and pray

- Praise God for being a real and powerful God who does not need to be supported by human hands, as do idols like Artemis or our favourite posessions.
- Thank God for Paul and the many others before and after him who are willing to risk imprisonment and affliction for the gospel of grace.
- Ask God to heal those around us who are ill, and pray that they would glorify him whether sick or well.

Endnote

1. FF Bruce, *The Book of Acts*, New International Commentary, rev. edn, Eerdmans, Grand Rapids, 1988, p. 360.

BIG TROUBLE IN JERUSALEM

[ACTS 21:17–26:32]

1. Imagine you are the apostle Paul, travelling to Jerusalem after your three missionary journeys. What sorts of emotions would you be experiencing?

In this study we rejoin Acts at a time of high tension and anticipation. The apostle Paul finally arrives in Jerusalem, despite many warnings that trouble awaits him there (e.g. 21:10-11). We, the readers, are full of nervous expectation. What will happen to Paul? He has faced opposition and hostility in virtually every other city he has visited—will the same fate await him in Jerusalem? Jesus was killed in Jerusalem—will the same thing happen to Paul?

With these sorts of questions in mind, we'll be covering quite a large section of Acts in this study. Much of our time will be spent simply reading the text. To try to streamline this process (as well as discover the recurring themes throughout these chapters), we'll be thinking about the same four basic questions as we read through each section at a time. (If you are doing this study in a group, you could divide into subgroups, each take one section and then report back to each other.)

Read Acts 21:17–22:29.

2. What events contribute to Paul having to give a defence of himself? What (if any) specific charges are made about him?

3. What does Paul say in his defence?

4. What reaction does Paul's defence have on his audience?

5. In what ways does this section highlight Paul's innocence?

You were expecting...?

SADLY, OUR WORST FEARS FOR PAUL come true. Paul's presence in the temple creates a mindless riot. The problem is that many Jews have failed to understand the gospel properly. Accusations are made that Paul is seeking to teach Jews to "forsake Moses", and not circumcise their children (21:21). However Acts has made it abundantly clear that the coming of Jesus Christ is the *fulfilment* of the Old Testament, rather than the undermining of the Old Testament.

(Remember Stephen's speech in Acts 7, and Paul's speech in Pisidian Antioch in Acts 13.) Certainly believers no longer *must* be circumcised in order to be one of God's people, but that's not to say that they can't be if they wish to. As we have already seen, Paul is very happy for circumcision to occur (16:3). The Jews, however, are beyond listening. As with their dealings with Jesus, their eyes are blinded by jealousy and pride.

Read Acts 22:30–23:35.

6. What events contribute to Paul having to give a defence of himself? What (if any) specific charges are made about him?

7. What does Paul say in his defence?

8. What reaction does Paul's defence have on his audience?

9. In what ways does this section highlight the blamelessness of Paul's actions?

Read Acts 24.

10. What events contribute to Paul having to give a defence of himself? What (if any) specific charges are made about him?

11. What does Paul say in his defence?

12. What reaction does Paul's defence have on his audience?

13. In what ways does this section highlight the blamelessness of Paul's actions?

Read Acts 25:1-22.

14. What events contribute to Paul having to give a defence of himself? What (if any) specific charges are made about him?

15. What does Paul say in defence of himself?

16. What reaction does Paul's defence have on his audience?

17. In what ways does this section highlight the blamelessness of Paul's actions?

Read Acts 25:23–26:32.
18. What events contribute to Paul having to give a defence of himself? What (if any) specific charges are made about him?

19. What does Paul say in defence of himself?

20. What reaction does Paul's defence have on his audience?

21. In what ways does this section highlight the blamelessness of Paul's actions?

The truth, the whole truth and nothing but the truth

IN THIS STUDY, WE HAVE DISCOV-
ered a recurring cycle of events. On five
different occasions, Paul is called to give
an account of his belief and actions.
Jesus' words about Paul are certainly
coming true: "He is a chosen instrument
of mine to carry my name before the
Gentiles and kings and the children of
Israel" (9:15). Luke devotes considerable
space to Paul's defence speeches. Clearly,
some important lessons are to be had
here. Several truths in particular need to
be noted.

a) The clarity and authority of Paul's calling

Paul's encounter with the risen Christ
plays a prominent role in several of
Paul's defences. Paul's apostleship to the
Gentiles, and the message he proclaimed, are not of his own making; they
come with all the authority of the Lord
Jesus Christ. As Paul says to the Galatians:

> For I would have you know, broth-
> ers, that the gospel that was

preached by me is not man's gospel.
For I did not receive it from any
man, nor was I taught it, but I
received it through a revelation of
Jesus Christ. (Gal 1:11-12)

b) The blamelessness of Paul

Closely related to the above point is the
clear fact that Paul is innocent of any
crime as he spreads the gospel of Jesus.
This is a truth that is acknowledged on
more than one occasion by those who
stand in judgement on Paul (e.g. 23:29,
26:30-32). This is also a truth that Luke
seems especially keen for us, the readers,
to be clear about. (Could it be that
Theophilus to whom Luke is writing
[1:1] is Paul's lawyer in Rome?)

c) The reasonableness of the gospel

We have already noted that Acts reflects the reasonableness of the gospel
(e.g. 17:1-12). This is again emphasized
in Paul's defences. Paul's words to Festus
are especially pertinent: "I am speaking
true and rational words" (26:25).

» Implications

(Choose one or more of the following to think about further or to discuss in your group.)

- Which of Paul's defences do you find the most compelling? Why? Are there any clues for us about how we might do our evangelism?

- If the gospel is "true and rational" (26:25), why is it that so many people don't believe it?

- What are some ways in which we can help people see that the news of Jesus is "true and rational"?

- What comfort is there for us in that Paul did not preach a man-made gospel?

- In what way is Paul an encouragement to us in this section of Acts?

» Give thanks and pray

- Praise God for being gracious enough to give us the beautiful news of the gospel, a divine plan worth more than any man-made comfort.
- Thank God that he is not absent when we are accused, but that instead he is with us as the one who is always faithful and concerned for justice, in control of both his people and their attackers.
- Ask God to protect Christians today who are on trial for their faith and evangelism, that the authorities over them would see the reason and truth behind their actions.

ROME OR BUST

[ACTS 27–28]

1. Is there a city or town that you have not visited before but would very much like to? Which city is it, and why would you like to go there?

In the time of the apostle Paul, all roads led to Rome. Rome was the centre and capital of the known world.

> Rome, the largest and most splendid of ancient cities, acted like a magnet to its peoples… Its buildings were famous—the three circuses and their daring chariot races, the palaces of the Caesars, the tombs of the illustrious dead, the temples (especially the Pantheon erected by Augustus), the basilicas, theatres, baths and aqueducts, and particularly the bustling forum, the hub of the city's commercial, social, political and religious life.[1]

And so it is that as Acts draws to a close, the apostle Paul draws closer to Rome. For if the gospel is to go "to the end of the earth" (1:8), it must go to Rome.

Re-read Acts 25:9-12.

2. From a human perspective, why is Paul on his way to Rome?

Read Acts 27:1-28:10.

3. Trace Paul's route on the map on page 51.

4. From the risen Christ's perspective, why is Paul on his way to Rome (27:24-25)? (Compare Acts 23:11.)

5. List the different ways in which we see God protecting Paul during his trip to Rome.

6. List the different ways in which Paul reveals himself to be a man of faith during his trip to Rome.

7. Acts 27:24 is the third time that God tells Paul to have courage and not be afraid (see also 18:9-10, 23:11). In each case, what is the task for which God is protecting Paul?

8. In the space of three verses, the sailors change their opinion of Paul from a murderer to a god (28:3-6)! What is Paul's opinion of himself (27:23)?

The invincible risen Christ

THROUGHOUT THESE STUDIES, WE have often paused to consider the invincibility and authority of the risen Christ. As early as 1:8, we noted that Christ's action plan is for the gospel to go to the end of the earth. We have discovered that nothing has been able to stop him in that plan. Hostile kings have been humbled and brought down (12:19-24), fierce persecutors have been transformed into faithful preachers (9:1-30), uneducated men have baffled the Jewish leaders (4:13-22) and even persecution has only served to spread the gospel further (8:1-4). The risen Christ is determined that men, women and children of all nations will hear the good news that "everyone who calls upon the name of the Lord shall be saved" (2:21).

The invincibility of the risen Christ also shines through in the apostle Paul's eventful journey to Rome. Luke's graphic description of Paul's trip reveals to us that neither human scheming, nor forces of nature, can thwart the purposes and plans of Christ. Over the last seven chapters, Paul has been caught up in a violent riot, falsely arrested, gone through numerous trials, had an ambush plotted against him, been caught in a violent storm at sea, almost thrown overboard, shipwrecked and bitten by a deadly snake. And still Paul arrives safe and sound in Rome! It is clear testimony to the power of the risen Christ. Ever since Paul's conversion, it has been Christ's plan that Paul should testify to kings in his name (9:15). For this very reason, Christ has planned for Paul to visit Rome (23:11)—and what the risen Christ plans, he accomplishes.

Read Acts 28:11-22.

9. What has reached Rome ahead of Paul (vv. 14-15)? What has not reached Rome ahead of Paul (v. 21)? How is this further evidence of God protecting Paul?

10. What does Paul mean when he says, "it is because of the hope of Israel that I am wearing this chain" (v. 20)?

Read Acts 28:23-31.

11. In verse 23, we're told that Paul tried to convince the Jews "about Jesus". What specific things about Jesus do you think Paul was trying to convince them of?

12. What response does Paul receive to his preaching in Rome (vv. 24-25)?

13. According to Isaiah 6, why are the Jews ever hearing but never understanding (v. 27)? How have we seen this in action in Acts?

14. In what ways do you think verses 30-31 form a fitting conclusion to the book of Acts?

When in Rome

HAVING STRESSED THE AUTHORITY of the risen Christ in Paul's trip to Rome, the events of Paul's preaching in Rome serve to emphasize two other important themes that we have already noted in Acts.

a) Rejection by the Jews

At the start of Acts, Jesus taught his disciples about the kingdom of God (1:3), and the disciples expected that the kingdom would eventually be given to Israel (1:6). Tragically, as Paul explains the kingdom of God to the Jews in Rome, it is now clear that the kingdom will not be restored to Israel at all. The response to Paul's preaching in Rome reaffirms what we have seen all along in Acts.

Israel has closed her heart, eyes and ears to the gospel. As Paul quotes Isaiah 6 (28:26-27), our minds are taken back to another event in Luke's first volume, when Jesus himself quoted the same text after the parable of the soils (Luke 8:10). Sadly, Israel has shown herself to be an unproductive, unfruitful soil.

b) Salvation to the Gentiles

One of the great themes of Acts has been that "everyone who believes in [Jesus] receives forgiveness of sins through his name" (10:43). By the grace of God, salvation is now available to all: Jew and Gentile alike. Again, this theme is celebrated at the close of the book. In the very last scene, we leave the apostle Paul welcoming *all* who came to see him (v. 30) and preaching without hindrance about the kingdom of God (v. 31).

And so the curtain is drawn on the book of Acts. It is a part of the word of God that should thrill us and challenge us because of what we have discovered about our Lord and Saviour—our *risen* Lord and Saviour. He cannot be stopped in his heart's desire for everyone to hear the good news of repentance, forgiveness of sins and the gift of the Holy Spirit.

All of which is enormously exciting—for the acts of the apostles may well have finished, but the acts of the risen Christ most definitely have not!

» Implications

(Choose one or more of the following to think about further or to discuss in your group.)

- Acts finishes with Paul preaching "with all boldness" in Rome. What sorts of things can stop us from being bold in our evangelism? How can we help each other be bolder than we sometimes are?

- Before Paul arrived at Rome he had already written them the letter known as Romans. In that letter he wrote:

  First, I thank my God through Jesus Christ for all of you, because your faith is proclaimed in all the world. For God is my witness, whom I serve with my spirit in the gospel of his Son, that without ceasing I mention you always in my prayers, asking that somehow by God's will I may now at last succeed in coming to you. For I long to see you, that I may impart to you some spiritual gift to strengthen you—that is, that we may be mutually encouraged by each other's faith, both yours and mine. I do not want you to be unaware, brothers, that I have often intended to come to you (but thus far have been prevented), in order that I may reap some harvest among you as well as among the rest of the Gentiles. I am under obligation both to Greeks and to barbarians, both to the wise and to the foolish. So I am eager to preach the gospel to you also who are in Rome.

For I am not ashamed of the gospel, for it is the power of God for salvation to everyone who believes, to the Jew first and also to the Greek. For in it the righteousness of God is revealed from faith for faith, as it is written, "The righteous shall live by faith". (Rom 1:8-17)

What do we learn here of Paul's desire for the Roman Christians prior to his arrival? What lessons can we draw from Paul's words?

- Is there any specific passage in Acts that has particularly challenged or comforted you? Which one was it, and why?

» Give thanks and pray

- Praise God for the salvation he offers through Jesus. Thank God that he was not willing to let us die in our sin as we deserve but instead sends the gospel to the nations through his word and his people, protecting them in amazing ways. It is an incredible gift from an incredible God.
- Spend some time giving thanks for those people whom the risen Christ has used to bring the gospel to you.
- Ask that our risen Lord may use you to take the gospel to others, not fearing opposition but trusting fully in him.

Endnotes
1. John Stott, *The Message of Acts*, Bible Speaks Today, IVP, Leicester, 1994, p. 383.